VIEW FROM THE TOP

by

George S. Keller
of the Michigan and Indiana Bars

A Small Town Veteran Trial Lawyer
Looks Back on 50 Years of
Courtroom Experience

Keller & Keller

VIEW FROM THE TOP

First Edition

Designed and printed by J&M Sandlin Bookmakers,
South Bend, Indiana

Rowan Tree Press
ISBN# 1-890103-00-4

VIEW FROM THE TOP

I dedicate these memoirs to my beautiful wife, Rachel, whose constant support permitted me to advance in the trial practice and whose affection and drive has always been a source of inspiration for me. I seldom went to a trial without her present in the spectator bench. I really strode the boards as much to persuade her, as the jurors, the merits of my cause. Her counsel, frequent criticism, and often keen and perceptive observation of trial events always influenced me.

VIEW FROM THE TOP

Contents

INTRODUCTION

The practice of law in the 1930's when I started, was a far cry from the practice of law today. I can relate only to small town practice. There were no specialties. If one graduated from a law school and had passed the bar, then not only in theory, but actually, he was expected to handle cases across the board, any area of the law. Patent law of course was sacrosanct to its practitioners. I thought myself competent to handle whatever was presented to me—criminal, tort, property, estate, tax, bankruptcy, worker's compensation, or whatever the problem. I was buoyed by a cocky self-appraisal, doubtless fostered by lack of experience, that I was competent and equal to any of the old trial masters. I was eager to test their mettle against mine in court conflict.

There were no trial seminars, advocacy institutes, strategy or tactics clinics, and certainly no continuing legal education institutes. A law school moot court session for one semester was the only sparse training. One had to learn trial strategy by doing and there simply was no substitute for the grueling experience of pitting oneself against experienced trial lawyers in the courtroom in order to win your "wings" and become a full-fledged trial advocate. It was an ordeal by fire and an exposure to be fully and enthusiastically embraced, if one sought any standing at the trial bar. Thus only could the fledgling attorney emerge as a recognized trial counsel to whom clients' causes might be entrusted. That exposure was shunned by many lawyers who preferred the cloistered protection of an office practice and engaged only in corporate, tax, probate or bank-

i

ruptcy matters.

I elected to go the trial route and therefore never had rapport with the type of practice limited to office consultations. That eagerness for trial practice secured me many trial opportunities in many states and allowed me several times to assay into areas of trial conflict, involving both large and small matters, to assert positions unique and novel in the law. The practice identified me personally with the lives and fortunes of my clients. I conceived this to be the noblest purpose of the legal profession, namely, to responsibly serve those clients who secured my representation to the hilt of my ability, without a great deal of concern for consequence.

There are few remaining of my contemporaries, certainly in the area of Southwestern Michigan, now practicing. Recognizing my era has passed and that young trial lawyers will find it interesting to compare their experiences and relate to the trial practitioners of my generation, I believe it would be useful to express, in the form of memoirs, my recollection of challenging cases in that era handled in a small town.

For the young attorney, the flavor and recall of the activity of that period may appear quaintly remote from the present. The America of the '30's, '40's, and '50's, was a remarkably changing era, one far simpler and more direct than the present, but withal beginning to stir and rouse itself and leave the period of depression, World War II and post-war-boom. It was an exciting time to practice law in a small community when often there were involved cases to which the entire population could relate. The attorney committed to a client's cause, often became perceived as a champion of a more universal cause, which could and did excite the sympathy and attention of a significant segment of the community.

These memoirs will relate to selected cases, all involving true fact issues and actual forums, many having the exciting and fascinating flavor of a fiction plot. They were the kind of cases presented to the young practicing attorney in a small community in the '30's, '40's, '50's and '60's who was willing to grapple and do battle for their resolution in the law courts. The text should be interesting to anyone curious how the concerns of small ordinary people can be addressed and redressed at any time by the American system of justice and resort to a court of law.

BACKGROUND

Attorney Charles Kavanagh died October 10, 1936. All the previous night and that early morning, I alone sat with him in vigil as his life ebbed and spent. I felt a devastating personal loss for I loved and respected him. Additionally, I had spent two years as a law clerk with him during my last two years of law school at Notre Dame. I had matriculated at the University of Michigan Law School in 1933 in the law class of 1936, which numbered many brilliant young men, one of whom was Mennen Williams, destined to be Governor of Michigan, and then ultimately supreme Court Justice of the Michigan Supreme Court. Without funds to support me I had to work my way through school that first year at Michigan. I also had to be separated from my wife who lived in Niles, Michigan, managing her father's magazine agency. We both felt the cruelty of the separation. Rachel had induced Charles Kavanagh to take me on as his law clerk if I transferred from Michigan to Notre Dame the last two years of my law study. This Kavanagh had done, enabling my wife and I to be together. For two years I hitchhiked from Niles to Notre Dame, Indiana, to complete my law program. The law clerkship, largely limited to collecting delinquent accounts, was a valuable assist to my concrete objective approach to the law for it familiarized me, while still a student, with the actual world in which law was practiced. I had done well with my law studies, having graduated among the top of my class at Notre Dame, and having been made an Associate Editor of the Notre Dame Law Review. I had looked forward to immediately getting involved with an older practitioner. I had taken the Indiana and Michigan Bar Examinations and was advised that I passed the Indiana examination, but when I sat by my dying mentors side, I had yet to be notified I had successfully passed the Michigan Bar Examination.

Mr. Kavanagh's death therefore came not only as a personal shock; literally, my expectations of an association addressed to a partnership with a practicing attorney, collapsed. Instead, I was confronted with the necessity of launching my career as a neophyte in a strictly solo operation.

Kavanagh's secretary, Bessie Pennell, who had been with him for 30 years, was the key asset in the office. I had somehow managed to scrape together $500 to buy Kavanagh's library equipment, desk and the remainder of the equipment, but I knew that I would not be able to long survive without the able assistance of this longtime capable legal secretary (Jay Mertz, the Supreme Court Reporter, apprised of my circumstances, advised me by phone that he had checked out the examination results and while the notification was not official, my score was sufficiently high and there would be no question I had passed the examination).

In my eagerness to retain Miss Pennell, I made her an astonishing offer. If she would remain with me I would give her one-half of all gross receipts and from my half of the receipts I would take care of all of the expenses, rent, supplies, publications, etc.! I could not assure her how long this would go on, but she agreed she would stay with me.

In the current era of equal rights for women, now prevalent, it will be interesting to the reader to relate not only this compact with my secretary, but also how our initial agreement that she continue with me came about. Bessie Pennell started with Charles Kavanagh as a legal secretary in the year 1903. As a young woman she had been going with a young man who had offered his hand in marriage. She was concerned how her employer would regard the prospect of a married woman working as a legal secretary. She knew only that married women simply did not, or should not, work out of the home, and certainly not as legal secretaries. In most offices of that era legal secretaries were old maids. Certainly young married mothers did not seek this kind of employment outside the home. Kavanagh made it very clear to Bessie that if she married her swain, he would not have her in the office. She made the difficult choice. She gave up marriage and continued as a legal secretary for Kavanagh for a period of 30 years until his death in October, 1936. From 1912 when Kavanagh moved from Berrien Springs, Michigan, to Niles, Michigan, until his death, she drove six days a week to and from Berrien Springs, her home, to Niles, in order to attend her duties. The neighbors could set their clocks on the time she left her home to come to work and when she returned. She was most faithful in the discharge of her duties and was a magnificent asset to her employer. As most legal secretaries in that day and the present were accustomed to doing, she became especially adept in probate matters, sufficiently so to be in total charge of all paper preparation.

Against that background, I must relate what happened when Kavanagh died and Bessie Pennell was first presented with the prospect of continuing her long employment with me as a young lawyer. Bessie related to me that the young man who had proposed marriage to her 30 years before, had raised his family, his wife had died and that, again single, he had approached her and offered marriage a second time. She said she wished to continue her career as a legal secretary, that it meant a great deal to her, and she wanted to know my reaction to her marriage to Mr. Smith. Would I agree that if she did marry she could continue as my legal secretary? She promised me the same devotion to detail and duty she had given to Kavanagh. Needless to say, I could not find it in my heart to deny her the comfort of marriage. After marriage she was as faithful and circumspect about her duties as she possibly could have been when single and employed by Kavanagh.

Such was the era then in the '30's. There were no married women, certainly not in Niles, Michigan, who were employed by other attorneys as legal secretaries. The day of the suffragist for women's equal rights had not yet fully dawned in America. It was true here and there an isolated woman doctor or woman lawyer held forth, but they were few and far between. It was indeed a man's world and a woman's place largely remained in the home.

The equipment in my office as I look back at it now was primitive. There were of course no computers and L.C. Smith was standard typewriter equipment. IBM was unknown. I was fortunate to have an old Dictaphone which employed a wax cylinder for dictation. The cylinder, in order to be reused, was shaved and so two pieces of equipment, namely the dictator and the wax cylinder shaver comprised my dictating equipment. The old Dictaphone equipment was used without benefit, as far as I know, of any service calls for some 20 years. Mr. Kavanagh had acquired the equipment in 1911 and had used it until his death.

BEGINNING CASES

The first prospect of any case that came into my office was that of a woman who wanted a divorce. The husband came in with her and advanced $67: $60 for attorney fees and $7 for costs. It seemed such a huge fee to me at the time that I was elated to have it, regardless somewhat nonplused by the fact the husband came in with his wife. The rule of collusion in that era was a strong one. Frankly, I did not know how to handle it. A further circumstance complicated my acceptance of the case. I had not yet been admitted to the Michigan bar though I had been advised by Reporter Mertz that my grades were sufficiently high and I would shortly receive my certificate of successful completion. I told the client that she would have to wait for a couple of weeks before I could file an action. She departed not knowing exactly why I put the matter off, but satisfied regardless. In the interim she was told by another attorney that I had not been yet admitted the bar. When she returned, I restored her money and wished her good luck.

Going through Kavanagh's files, I found one case immediately that piqued my interest. A New York stockbroker had a claim against Lawrence Plym, a leading industrialist in town who was the owner of

Kawneer Company (later bought out by American Metal Climax Company). It appeared that Mr. Plym had stock in a big bank corporation during the depression and he had transferred it to the name of his stockbroker for the purpose of sale. Before it could be sold a double assessment was levied which required the owner of the stock to pay a substantial sum to help cover the bank's debts. This double assessment occurred while the stock was in the name of the stockbroker prior to sale. He made claim against Plym and the latter took the arrogant position this was one of the risks a stockbroker took by virtue of his occupation. Since the stock was in the broker's name at the time of the assessment, he, the broker and not Plym, must assume the risk of assessment.

The claim had been referred for collection to Kavanagh because of his membership in the Commercial Law League of America which was a referring service for collections. Kavanagh had failed for a period of some six months to take any action on it and for good reason. Mr. Plym was the owner of the biggest and most powerful corporation in the community, the Kawneer Corporation, which was on the big board and manufactured store fronts and doors which were marketed all over the world. He was also the owner and publisher of the Niles Daily Star, the local newspaper, and he wielded a very large significant influence and power in the community. It was said of him that he had a long-lasting memory and if anyone earned his wrath, he was certain to feel it. I looked at the file and felt strongly that Plym owed the stockbroker the amount of the assessment and it was grossly unfair he should avoid his liability. Without any great hesitation, I drafted my declaration in Circuit Court and promptly had the papers filed and the process served upon the local magnate. Other attorneys who heard of the incident thought I was a brash youngster. Attorney Edwin Donahue, one of the old tigers of the bar, told me in confidence he would not have touched the matter with a ten foot pole. Circuit Judge Charles White, of whom it was said not a single decision had ever been reversed on appeal, had lost the election to the circuit bench in November, 1936. He reentered private practice with Stuart B. White, no relation, but father of Circuit Court Judge

William S. White. He was retained by Plym to represent him.

During the summer of 1936, I had taken an active interest along with and because of the urging of Charles Kavanagh, in soliciting support for Fremont Evans' bid to the Circuit Court bench and was positive I had secured a significant number of votes. Evans won the election by the small margin of six votes. I felt therefore a sense of exhilaration with the prospect of having the eminent Judge White as counsel for Plym in what I expected to be a jury trial on the Circuit Court level. At that time, the Kawneer corporate affairs and legal business in Niles, Michigan, were subject to being transferred periodically from the Burns-Hadsell Firm to the White and White firm, the two most prestigious firms in the City of Niles and in the County of Berrien. Judge White's retirement from the bench and his joining with Stuart White in the firm of White and White encouraged I am sure the transfer of the Plym business to the latter firm. Needless to say, I was bitterly disappointed that Judge White counseled his client, probably to the latter's displeasure to settle the case rather than take it to court, certainly before a jury. I took no pleasure in taking a consent judgment, feeling I was deprived of the opportunity to test my budding forensic skills against eminently qualified Plym counsel. However, the taste for battle and the flavor of the contest were making themselves felt for me and I began to have a tremendous interest in the actual trial of cases and literally sought out opportunities to go to Court.

One such experience of mine occurred in Cassopolis, Michigan, a small community east of Niles in Cass County. I had been six months at the bar and represented a little country girl who had driven her old four door Buick into an intersection and collided with a taxicab. The Defendant taxicab operator was represented by Attorneys Asa Hayden and Ulysses P. Eby, whose combined experience at the trial bar exceeded 75 years. I was thrilled at the prospect of the contest for it was my first experience in a Circuit Court trial situation. It was a tradition then, as it is now, that a lawyer should win his first case and I was determined to stay with the tradition. A jury of twelve panelmen contained at least four who were volunteer firemen. It was not uncommon in that period at least once during the trial of a cause that there be a fire. This happened in my case and the four volunteer firemen had to quickly excuse themselves, causing the trial to be suspended until they returned. I strode the boards in a manner that probable aped both Asa Hayden and Ulysses P. Eby who came from an era of the law as remote to me then as the current is to my era in the 30's. I recall vividly that the tilting point in the entire examination and cross-examination of the young girl plaintiff was a question placed to her on cross-examination by Attorney Eby:

Q: Tell me Miss Engles, give me your best estimate of how much your automobile weighed?

Miss Engles pondered the question, deliberated, hesitated, and then she gave her answer:

A: I would suspect around 500 pounds.

The jurors laughed, I laughed, and the defense attorneys laughed. The car actually was a heavy 4500 pounds. My whole argument, as I recall now, was that the credibility of the Plaintiff had been thoroughly tested by defense counsel and found worthy of belief as to how the accident occurred. She told it the way it was, the way she believed it was, and her answer of 500 pounds, was a wholly frank, guileless and honest answer, wholly at odds with any suggestion that she would consciously or otherwise exaggerate or misrepresent her recollection of any incident involved in the accident. The jury awarded verdict for something less than $300 to the Plaintiff and I experienced my first sense of exhilaration that comes to the trial attorney when he achieves a successful result for his labors.

On sober reflection, now 50 years from the event, one must concede that the argument could effectively be made that the credibility of a witness who makes such disparate judgment or estimate surely may be questioned in regard to the accuracy of other observations and testimony relating to fact matters.

Attorney Kavanagh had confided to me while I was his law clerk that after 30 years in the practice, after paying his secretary $20 per week, rent of $20 per month, publications, supplies and miscellaneous expenses, he was able to net $50 per week for himself. Somehow this satisfied me that the practice of law would be sufficiently rewarding to support a wife and family. It must be recalled that the country was in the throes of a deep depression. Milk was 10 cents a quart, eggs were 10 cents a dozen. Unemployed men sought out a substance by selling apples on the streets for 5 cents. The most elegant home in Niles was the Carmi Smith home on Main Street across from the City Hall. It was rumored that Smith, a retired lumberman who was one of my clients as a supplier of delinquent accounts for collection, had lavished the sum of $10,000 on the structure.

As it turned out, my first full year of practice did net me $2,500, so Kavanagh's estimate of potential earnings were right on mark. Probate cases, corporate, banking and substantial real estate practice did not come my way, for the established firms of Burns-Hadsell and White and White had banking and corporate business all tied up. Probate files were developed by attorneys of long-standing who had drafted wills for old clients, the originals of which they closely guarded in their safes. Casper Grathwohl who commenced practice in 1929, was to hang on to the City Attorney's position in Niles for so long that I lost heart in ever having a try at it. As a lone solo practitioner and newcomer to the small community of Niles, about the only type of case I attracted were divorces and delinquent account collections, the latter of which I used as frequently as I could to involve myself in litigation in the Justice of the Peace Courts. These Courts were really the pits, where the young attorney could and did, if he wished to advance in the trial field, secure practice for his forensic skills. The days of such courts were numbered, for in the '60's, the J.P. system was outlawed.

The Niles bar was a proud and active one and prided itself on having the best trial lawyers, or at least as good trial lawyers as practiced in Berrien County, or elsewhere. Wilbur Burns was the first president of the integrated Michigan State Bar and he was an eminently qualified and scholarly lawyer who was regarded by all with respect as the

Dean of the Niles Bar in the '30's. His partner, Philip A. Hadsell, later to be elevated to the Circuit Court bench, was equally well regarded as a topflight lawyer. Stuart B. White, father of the now retired Circuit Court Judge, William S. White, was considered among the most forceful, skillful and successful lawyers in the State of Michigan. When he was joined by Judge Charles White after the latter's retirement from the Circuit Court bench, the firm of White and White was a legal adversary in any case calculated to challenge the best effort of a trial lawyer anywhere.

Then there was Edwin Donahue, Sr., a real heavyweight trial lawyer who handled with great skill and acumen some of the most litigious issues of the area. These were the standout trial lawyers with whom the younger men at the bar had to contend. After I opened a solo practice, Harold Klute joined with Edwin Donahue for awhile and then swung over to White and White. Andrew Mollison joined the Burns-Hadsell firm. Their futures, tied to these prestigious firms, were assured. I had no doubt of mine though it seemed for too long to be limited to divorces and small Justice of the Peace Court cases.

Divorces and My Reaction

There was a period when I was doing over 75 divorces a year. They indeed did supply for me a major part of my income. There came a time, probably in the late '40's, when I began to see divorce, especially where children were involved, as evil and a dirty part of the practice of law. I saw children being literally orphaned and losing both parents in ugly quarrels over custody, and I envisioned the breakup of the home, the seeds being sown of juvenile delinquency which would later plague society. My concern deepened and I progressed through two periods.

Initially my observation was that most, indeed probably all divorces, were initiated by wives. This caused me to be determined to reject representation of divorce cases, unless it be on behalf of the husband, who would agree to vigorously defend the action and save the marriage. In the alternative, I would spend countless hours trying to counsel couples and accomplish their reconciliation with each other. I recall it became well known in the Community of Niles that I had taken this course and generally I was ridiculed. The general comment was that if I did not handle this kind of case, it was simply my loss and other lawyers would take these cases and I would substantially lose the fees

7

involved. Actually, it worked differently. I became involved with divorce trial litigation, than which there is nothing more strident and litigious. A typical case occurred in the early '50's. A man came to me who had agreed to let his wife proceed with her divorce with another lawyer. He had consented to her taking custody of the children and receiving the whole of their real estate. His distress was provoked primarily because during their separation and his removal from the home it had come to his attention that a supposedly good friend of his had in fact cuckolded him and was having an affair with his wife. Worse, he was known to be sleeping and cohabiting with his wife in their bedroom.

The man's anger was intense and he asked me my advice. I shared his wrath and told him: "I would shoot the S.O.B." The client was shocked and I calmed him down ultimately to say: "I mean with camera and flashbulbs." The husband told me how his home was located and the position specifically of the bedroom windows which remained open with screens and he further told me that he retained the key to the front door of the residence. I detailed the strategy as a squad leader would to his men in course of combat: "Arrive stealthily at 11:30 tonight, position yourself with camera at the ready by the open bedroom and when you hear the bedsprings creak, break through the screen and start snapping flash pictures like mad, all the while your father, having unlocked the front door, enters and prevents any escape." The client was appropriately impressed and enthused with a battle plan worthy of his best effort.

The next day he came back highly flushed with a roll of undeveloped film which produced pictures of unusual clarity and detail. These would prove of good value in later satisfying a Circuit Court Judge, who ordinarily would have bent every rule to presume the wife to be the fit guardian of the minor children, but instead ruled in favor of the contesting father. The developed pictures demonstrated that upon entering his home, the irate husband had stripped the bed covering from his marital bed and from the foot of the bed there was shown the picture of his wife, in the nude, derriere skyward, with a man, nude except for a wristwatch clearly showing on the left hand, leaping out of the bed. The wrist watch showed the hour of 11:30. How closely had my client followed instructions!

Another picture frame demonstrated the nude male friend in the closet confronted by the husband with flash camera. The man had the wit, withal poorly placed to say: "Guess what I am waiting for? A streetcar!"

It was not long into the '50's that I took a pledge never again to handle a divorce case on either side, and this for the reason alone that I was personally convinced, whether or not advisedly from another's viewpoint, that such actions stirred up and promoted much more evil, trouble and emotional maladjustment of all the parties involved, including the children, than any compensating benefit attained.

I was to be sorely tested in this matter by a very good friend of mine, a prominent physician in the Niles area. He and I would have done any favor for the other without any thought of recompense. He and his wife had some emotional differences which ultimately developed to a point where they were irreconcilable and I had spent countless hours trying to reconcile them for the sake of their two adopted children for a period approximating ten years. When the wife, in a rage, threw a knife narrowly missing the doctor, the latter gave up and sought my assistance for a divorce.

The doctor did not understand my position. I would not represent him in a divorce action because of the circumstance that I had taken the pledge with myself. Actually, I have to admit that I had trouble reconciling to my inability to help him in his request. He was to blame me for literally keeping a fouled up marriage going for ten miserable years by my counseling. I had no real answer except to refer his case to a prominent attorney in the St. Joseph area who successfully was to conclude a bitter court struggle. The charge of $15,000 in fees, a very high figure at that time, was resented by my friend. The most I could do was to demand a referral fee of one-third thereof and rebate to him $5,000 of the fee.

Simplicity Sit Down Strike and the Creation of the Independent Union

An event occurred in Niles in the late '40's that critically shaped my practice. A rash of sit down strikes had occurred about the country promoted by the C.I.O. in its competition with the more moderate A.F.L. The C.I.O. was sponsoring a rash of radical maneuvers whereby the membership was encouraged to take over a plant and sit down in it instead of routinely picketing on the outside to enforce their demands. A sit down strike occurred at the Simplicity Plant in Niles, the headquarters of the large women's clothing patterns company.

Niles had a number of key corporations located within its limits. Kawneer, National Standard and Simplicity were the three largest. Legal representation of these and smaller concerns was the preserve of established law firms. I, however, had occasion to strongly criticize the radical tactics of the C.I.O. group at Simplicity and when asked, I denounced the group and disclaimed any sympathy for it in its maneuver.

One day to my surprise while the sit down was still in effect, a group of about 24 men and women came to my office and introduced themselves to me as Simplicity employees. Jumping to conclusions, I told them quickly I had no interest in them and resented the radical take-over. The group burst out laughing and a Mrs. Burroughs, later to prove a strong spokeswoman for the group, spoke up and said they had come to me because they believed I would be the appropriate person to represent the group. They too resented the radical tactics of the C.I.O. and wanted my advice on how to form an independent union.

I was enthused with their reaction because it mirrored my own and confirmed it from the vantage point of a worker inside the plant. I proposed the formation of an independent union.

It was critical when created that the independent union be not perceived a creature of the company. A dummy company union plotted by the corporation to confuse and befuddle the employees would be a fraud. Such a phony union would deny them an honest, aggressive and truly independent vehicle with which to confront management on griev-ances, work rules, pay disputes and labor contracts. They had no experi-ence in labor matters and I did not wish to become a union/labor attorney though it had come to my attention that such representation did accom-plish, as an aside, solicitation of many legal issues from union members. I knew that any national union, certainly the C.I.O. would immediately charge us with being a company stooge, a company union and in any proceedings before it, inevitably the National Labor Relations Board would center on that charge and its reputed bias. It was determined the independent union, if I had anything to do with it, would be truly inde-pendent.

I incorporated the group with the Michigan Corporations and Se-curities Commission under the name of "Independent Association Patternmakers, Inc.." We set up by-laws, officers, and committees with all the trappings of a corporation. The Independent Union, the only one to my knowledge obtaining corporate status in the State of Michigan certainly, was put into the position of dealing on behalf of its membership, vis-a-vis the employer, Simplicity Corporation, on an equal corporate status.

The response of Simplicity workers, given a choice between their own and a radical national union, was quick and spontaneous. A dues and initiation schedule was set up involving a $1 initiation fee and 25 cents per month dues and shortly over 800 members were counted in our ranks. I was made counsel for the independent association and for several years I was to regularly attend monthly meetings, whereat labor matters, disputes and grievances were freely discussed. My fees of $25 per month was small pay for my efforts but over a period of some three to four years I was intimately to live the labor concerns and very often the life problems incurred by these members, to form friendships and contacts among the union members from whom I secured many clients.

A full labor contract was negotiated with the corporation wherein seniority, grievance structure and procedures through stewards, wage scales and other matters commonly subject to labor concern were delineated. Grievances, when presented, were vigorously prosecuted through the various stages by the appointed union grievance stewards to resolution. The independent character of the association at all times was sought to be maintained.

At the monthly meetings since there were involved some 800 employees, most of them female. It frequently happened that there would be problems related to pregnancies. The union often voted out of its meager treasury, expenditures for doctors and hospitals to the benefit of union members. There were also arranged picnics and beauty queen contests and other entertainment. In those days a 25 cent monthly dues schedule covered many benefits for the workers.

All of this was to come only after a noisy National Labor Relations Board hearing in which the C.I.O. made its expected charge that our union was in fact a stooge to the Simplicity Corporation, a dummy 'company union' designed to confuse, befuddle and betray the employees and deny them the benefit of honest, vigorous big national union representation such as the C.I.O. alone could provide and guarantee to compel management to buckle under to labor demands.

I discovered then something about my nature. If, and only if, I felt strongly about a client's cause was I able to vigorously, even angrily, articulate that position in a manner which would command attention, respect and often grudging acceptance. The board referee was to find that we were not in fact a company union, and the C.I.O. had not sustained their position. In the ensuing election, we won handily.

There ensued an era of troubled peace over several years, during which the union, acting under its contract with the corporate employer, pursued its objectives to represent the membership in all matters, advance grievances and responsibly discharge its duties as the bargaining representative of the employees. Sad to relate, the independent association could not long survive repeated onslaughts by the large national union. Some time early in the 1950's, another election was called at a time when our treasury was down to a bare $100. The C.I.O. had amassed a huge war chest for the local election. We could only fire one salvo when we could see the 'whites' if the enemy's' eyes. In a paper which was circulated to every member on the work force, we in detail answered the C.I.O. charges that we were a stooge company union. We had represented union members in the adjustment of their grievances, provided representation of all matters before the company, and negotiated a written contract and agreement with the company. In addition, we had contributed human and financial help to members in need, all within the bounds or our resources. All this was done without paying huge per capita charges to a national union. It was not enough and we were swept out of existence. The mood of the workers nationally and locally was to join with a big union and the C.I.O. was gathering its forces all across the country.

Trial Advocacy in the Courts as Lawyer's Best Advertisement of His Merits

In the current climate, it appears appropriate to some lawyers to use media advertisement. The Supreme Court decision which authorized advertisement of legal services in various media including television, radio and newspaper, has resulted in doctors, dentists and other professionals, as well as lawyers, routinely advertising their skills in magazines, telephone books, newspaper ads, radio and television. Not so in the earlier simpler days of the '40's, '50's and '60's. Solicitation by such means was on par with "ambulance chasing" and our ethics strictly forbade it.

There was always an appropriate and wholly acceptable technique of advancing one's image as an aggressive, articulate and capable fighter for a cause. When a client seeks out a lawyer, he ordinarily has a vital personal cause to entrust to him. In 1948, I had purchased the old

Buchanan house immediately south of the Four Flags Hotel on Fourth Street and had constructed a new handsome limestone office facility, which wrapped around the front of the old residence which had been the scene of a celebrated murder years before. It was the first use of an office in Niles by any lawyer on the first floor level. It was keenly believed that first floor premises on the Main Street should be reserved for mercantile purposes. I somehow escaped criticism because my office was located at 111 North Fourth Street, approximately 75 feet south of Main Street. I was across from the Post Office and in the center of the community. I was in a position to be seen and reckoned with by the older firms.

Cases came to my attention. One of the earliest had a strong effect upon me.

Helen Robb was a beautiful young girl who had taken up an illicit relationship with a local small industrialist. The latter had a wife and a number of children but that did not stop him from playing fast and loose with young Helen. One early morning in the late '40's they were returning from a bar west of Niles in the man's car. He was driving eastbound on M-60, and the car ran off the road and overturned. Helen was pinned under the vehicle, badly injured. During the course of a long hospitalization, she was to suffer the amputation of both legs above the knees. Her life was shattered and I was asked to represent her. Obviously this was a vital cause to which I had committed myself.

The industrialist came out of the accident with no significant injury and it was his claim that an opposing westbound truck had forced him off the highway and then left the scene of the accident. Helen seemed to have little recall of the accident. The man had $5,000 liability coverage with the Michigan Auto Club which was the usual coverage of that day and he personally had few tangible assets.

A very large legal impediment loomed. Michigan, as did most states of that era, had a guests/passenger statute which barred guests/passengers in an automobile from recovering money damages from their host driver unless the latter was guilty of "gross willful and wanton negligence." Unless it could be shown there was some payment or benefit flowing from passenger to driver incidental to the transportation of the former, the passenger's cause was doomed. It was necessary for the passenger to prove in effect that the driver intended to kill, maim or injure him. It was a terrible obstacle to overcome and liability carriers for negligent drivers had a field day in passenger/guest cases. Attorneys for the guest/passenger in those cases never expected to recover more than $500 nuisance or cost of defense evaluation.

The adjuster for AAA was a young man named Eugene Fields, who had settled a number of auto cases with me but never a guest / passenger claim, and he took the position that he never would settle a guest/passenger for other than a nuisance value. He ridiculed the Robb case and reminded me that this kind of claim was nickel and dime stuff and he made the expected maximum offer of $500. I told Fields that I was going to insist on the full $5,000 coverage plus an equal amount from the driver who had not been charged criminally in the matter and who had escaped injury-free. I strongly felt this man should somehow be made to pay some monies to Helen Robb for her very tragic injuries. Fields went on to say that he admired my spunk and that if I could "pull this one off, he was going to take up the law himself."

I determined to meet the challenge. Helen Robb and I reviewed her entire relationship with her paramour. The man had repeatedly esquired her to various bars, returning her late in the evening, and early in the morning to her home, promising her nothing but the questionable pleasure of his company. His wife, who had to know of the arrangement, adamantly refused to bring divorce proceedings. Helen was in a no win situation and she knew it.

As I drafted the Declaration to be filed in the Berrien County Circuit Court, Helen Robb was able to corroborate, support and have rapport with the allegations that I had inserted. I knew she would make, in her grossly crippled condition, an enormously effective witness and that if we could somehow muster the wherewithal to pass the scrutiny of the "gross, willful and wanton negligence standard" of the guest/passenger statute and get the case beyond the motion to direct, and safely lodge it with the jury, the latter had to find substantial damages for us.

The Declaration portrayed the stark and grim picture of a married philanderer, returning after bar hours, alone in his car with a frustrated, lonely and much used young woman who had been treated as a pawn for his pleasure, and for whom the relationship had now paled. He in turn was confronted by the hopelessness of his own married status and the abysmal emptiness he was offering poor Helen. He started to carelessly weave his car at high speed from one side to the other of the two lane highway on which his was the only vehicle. Helen was perturbed and she turned to him and said: "What are you doing?" The man replied, half in jest, half seriously: "There is no other way out, I am going to hell and I am going to take you with me." Helen in fright protested and reached over to turn off the ignition, at which time the philandering husband pushed her violently with his right arm and slammed her into the right door, in the process losing control of the automobile which overturned off the highway, tragically injuring, maiming and permanently crippling Helen. Thus was framed Helen's cause of action against the philanderer. Every complaint—complaints in those days were denominated Declarations—must set forth a scenario or script of the cause of action and any attorney, like a playwright, must set up the copy for later enactment of the drama for the judge and jury.

The case was filed in Court and was never tried, I must say to my disappointment. I had given a copy of the complaint to Fields and told him I wanted the full $5,000 coverage from the insurer and an equal contribution from the philandering defendant. I stated that in the context of the credibility of the latter, who claimed that an opposing vehicle had forced him off the highway and then fled the scene of the accident, and the Plaintiff Helen Robb, who had tragically suffered so much, the philanderer would suffer short shrift from the jury. I further said I did not believe the Defendant would have the chutzpah, with his wife and children in the Courtroom, to confront us in open court. Fields was ultimately to agree and the case was settled on my terms. How far from the present have damages progressed for the catastrophic injury! The case of Helen Robb today would not conceivably, unless the attorney handling it were to brook malpractice, settle for than less than 30 times, probably many more times, the modest amount I had concluded it on. But today the guest/passenger rule no longer prevails in Michigan and most states, and disability insurance limits are commonly $500,000 or $1,000,000.

Helen Robb was a survivor. She opened an answering service in Niles, one of the first for physicians in the area, and she was able to cheerfully serve in that capacity for many years until her death. She would often call me on the telephone and relate her experiences and I always felt a concern for her and had the satisfaction of having served in some small measure to accomplish her rehabilitation.

Eugene Fields, true to his prediction, eventually graduated from the University of Michigan Law School and for many years had a uniquely affluent practice in Kalamazoo, Michigan.

José Sierra vs. Daisy Minnear

In 1952, the affair of Daisy Minnear, a woman in her late fifties, with her young Mexican farmhand, 21 years of age, was a titillating gossip item of club women in Niles, Michigan. That gossip, related to me by members of a book club to which Mrs. Minnear belonged, made known to me the plight of José Sierra, long before I represented him.

Daisy and her invalid husband owned a 77-acre fruit farm in the Niles area. There was much work and many chores to perform, both on the farm and inside the house and buildings. Additionally, the care of her invalid husband was a heavy chore for her, and she required her farm-hands to assist her.

In July of 1949, José Sierra first came to the vicinity of Niles. He was one of those Mexican wetbacks who walked across the dry bed of the Rio Grande River into the United States from Mexico, and, following the crops as an itinerant worker, drifted north. He was illiterate and could not speak English, but he was young, strong and had good looking Latin features. As he trudged along the road past the Minnear farm, Daisy saw his trim, athletic, young frame, and she beckoned to him. By pantomime and finger gestures, she communicated she would pay him $7 a day for a seven-day week. She showed him around the farm and the house, introduced him to her husband and his needs. The boy began a course of literally indentured labor which was to extend for several years and involve him intimately with Daisy Minnear.

From July 4, 1949, until Mr. Minnear died on April 14, 1952, José cultivated, plowed and disked the fields, sprayed, trimmed and picked the fruit trees, and attended to the farm chores. He maintained the tractors and the farm equipment and repaired the farm buildings. He built walkways and concrete driveway, kept the premises in trim and was at Daisy's beck and call. His hours were long: from 7a.m. to late at night, seven days a week. His services extended to being a houseboy. He helped prepare the meals, washed and ironed the clothes. His chores included attending the bedridden, paralyzed husband until the latter's death , turning him in his bed, massaging and washing him and attending his most intimate needs. It seemed the call on him for service was endless. He performed many personal chores for Daisy—washing her hair, bathing her, trimming her nails and doing other services. By this time, the two of them had become lovers as well as employer-employee.

When the husband died, Daisy asked José to continue working for her, all on her promise to pay him the reasonable value of his services. She had a veritable paragon of labor-intensive service, and she wished him to stay. In November of 1952, Daisy took José on a vacation to his native Mexico. There she married him on November 16. The union was not to last long. she divorced him a few months later in February, 1953 in Berrien Circuit Court. Daisy had purchases all new clothing for her husband, and she had paid all of the expenses for the short vacation, but for all of his Herculean labors, she had paid him naught but $13 for the first two days of his labor and the sum of $700 shortly after the death of her husband.

In the divorce proceedings, Attorney Philip Hadsell, later to be elevated to the Circuit Bench of Berrien County, Michigan, represented Mrs. Minnear, and Chester Byrns, then a young lawyer, associated with the Benton Harbor law firm of Butzbaugh & Page, represented José Sierra. The decree left the Mexican youth with nary a dime, stranded except for his newly acquired wardrobe. He was highly incensed. Daisy's turkey was coming home to roost.

He sought me out at my Niles office and told me his tale of woe, to which I was able to relate because of the widely circulated gossip in the community. The youth was extremely bitter and complained in his broken English that he had unsparingly given of his extensive labors to a woman who had literally scammed him. His clothes were in tatters and deplorably nondescript.

I asked him about all the new clothing Daisy had lavished on him in Mexico, and his response was startling. He brought out a hunting knife and told me that with it he had gone through his closet and ripped all of his clothes to shreds. The destruction of his clothes was a symbolical act. He plainly wanted to turn the knife on Daisy. Here was a cause I felt impelled to champion somehow. This woman had taken cruel advantage of an illiterate youth!

I called on Chester Byrns, his attorney in the recent divorce action. Chester was a brilliant young lawyer, a recent Michigan law graduate with high honors. A Coif Honorary Society pin dangled from his vest. As he talked, he was the picture of a competent young attorney, securely associated with a prestigious Benton Harbor law firm, whose future at the Bar was assured. He was to be elevated to the Berrien bench on which he served with great distinction until his retirement in 1985. His opinions and court administration were of the highest caliber. In the view of his fellows at the Bar, he was generally regarded as Berrien's best bid to the Supreme Court. I always had some regret that Chet did not remain active in the ranks of the trial bar. He would have distinguished himself there as an advocate of the highest order.

Byrns was not particularly enthused with the Mexican youth's cause of action. My enthusiasm for an uncertain cause with only a contingency fee for the lawyer to reward his services, did not ignite more than a small reflecting ardor on his part. It was agreed I would handle the pleadings and the trial, and if it came to an appeal, which seemed more than likely, Byrns would apply himself thereto.

Complaint was filed in the Circuit Court in early 1954, and a bill of particulars was included to set forth in detail the many labors and services the young man had performed from July 4, 1949, until the marriage of the two on November 16, 1952, all at Daisy's request and promise to pay him the reasonable worth or *quantum meruit* of those services. $12,965 less credit for cash payments of $713 resulted in a net sum claimed of $12,252.

The trial opened before Berrien Circuit court Judge Tom Robinson on June 15, 1954. It was the shortest trial I had ever been in and the only time I can recall that an opposing attorney moved and secured a dismissal of my cause of action on my opening statement. I had related all the facts in José's cause with a passion I truly felt in the justice of his case against a conniving woman who had ruthlessly cheated him of the value of his labors. She had used him as a pawn until she tired of him and he no longer served her purposes, and then she had cast him aside as a spoiled child would discard a toy with which he had become annoyed. She had carried on a brazen affair with him before her husband's death, and thereafter she had lavished clothes on him to make him a suitable escort on a vacation trip to Mexico, culminating with a marriage there which lasted a short two and a half months. After the divorce, she had sent him packing, his labors for a long three and a half years unpaid. This debt ought not so blithely be palmed off by a scheming evil woman.

Philip Hadsell was an excellent trial attorney. He was shortly to become the next sitting Berrien judge. Of him his senior partner, Wilbur Byrns, the first president of Michigan's Integrated Bar, had said: "Give Phil the facts, and he will apply the law."

After I finished my opening statement, Hadsell arose to his feet and demonstrated that legal acumen (from the record):

Mr Hadsell: "Will counsel agree to the pretrial stipulation of fact regarding the joint ownership of Mr. and Mrs. Minnear during the time the Plaintiff worked on the farm until Mr.

Minnear died April 14, 1952?"

Mr. Keller: "Agreed."

Mr. Hadsell: "Plaintiff has admitted he was married to Daisy Minnear in Mexico on or about November 16, 1952, and they were divorced in February 1953. That is stipulated."

The jury was then excused, and Hadsell made motion for dismissal on two grounds: (1) Plaintiff's labors were performed to April 14, 1952, the date of Mr. Minnear's death, a time when Daisy Minnear was a married woman, incapable of contracting anything except for her separate estate, and (2) any obligation incurred after April 14, 1952, until November 16, 1952, when the two were married, during which time Daisy was single, was discharged as a matter of law by Daisy's marriage to José.

In a two-part motion, Philip Hadsell had struck me down. Circuit Judge Tom Robinson found Hadsell's affirmative defense of the marriage controlling as a matter of law. Daisy's obligation to José for any debt incurred before the marriage was declared canceled and extinguished by the marriage and Daisy released from any obligation.

Judge Robinson quoted ancient common law which he ruled was the law of Michigan until changed by legislation. He turned aside my argument that a liberal view should be taken of the effect of the married woman's act which is in derogation of the common law. He ruled that the marriage of the parties on November 16, 1952, extinguished whatever debt preexisted, and he proceeded to instruct the jury to remain in their chairs and to bring back a verdict of no cause. They did.

José Sierra was devastated. His plan to return to his native Mexico with some small savings was crushed. Byrns agreed to go forward as planned with the appeal to the Supreme Court. Grounds of the appeal briefly were that the Circuit court had erred in directing the verdict and in ruling that the married woman's act of Michigan, though rendering a married woman *sui juris*, that is, able in her own right to contract, did not abrogate and revoke any common law rule that might have preexisted the enactment ot the effect that marriage extinguished a pre-marital debt of the wife to the husband. A final error urged was that the Court failed to find that the divorce removed the disability of the husband to sue the wife for a pre-marital debt by her to him owed.

I looked forward with Byrns to the resolution of the appeal by the Supreme Court, for I believed the law should give redress to the Mexican youth. Jose was despondent and would receive no encouragement from me. He paid us neither fee nor costs adv anced. While the appeal was pending, he came to my office in Niles and told me of his despair receiving anything. He had parked his old decrepit automobile in front of my office, and he was leaving it there for me as some small recompense for what I had tried to do for him. He was going to go back to Mewxico the way he came, walking. I expressed my hope the Supreme Court would reverse the Trial Court, and if that occurred, how was I going to reach him? I was as frustrated as he, but he wouldn't listen, and against my protest, left my office and never returned. I didn't take the car. It was impounded by the local police as an abandoned vehicle.

The Supreme Court of Michigan in 1954 was not a liberal court. It routinely affirmed Judge Robinson's Circuit Court ruling, word for word (Sierra vs. Minnear, 341 Mich 182). Circuit Court opinion had become the Supreme Court's last word. Newspapers statewide carried the story prominently in headlines: "GIRLS, MARRY YOUR CREDITOR AND THEN DIVORCE HIM." It was a new twist that had not occurred to the popular mind.

The American Law Reports picked up the case for annotation where it found its niche as a dubious precedent for lawyers research (45 ALR 2nd 718).

José Sierra never knew how his appeal terminated. His lack of faith in it was, however, fully deserved.

THE NILES DEBATE ON THE CITY MANAGER FORM OF GOVERNMENT AS AN ASSIST

In the '50's, Casper Grathwhol, who had been the City Attorney since 1930, was replaced by Harold Klute. There was a time when I had hoped to be considered for the post but this was long past. Niles was one of the few communities in excess of a population of 15,000 anywhere in Michigan, and the only one in Berrien County which held onto the "weak mayor-council" form of government. A group advocating a change claimed that communities like Buchanan and St. Joseph had a more competent and efficient city management form which retained the services of a trained professional manager to control and determine the affairs of the community, in the manner of a corporate plant manager. Klute was strongly in favor of a revision which he said would bring Niles into the 20th Century and promote the best interests of the community. The then current mayor, Jerome Wood, had initially favored a revision, but because the Board of Public Works, which was a very big and substantial segment of the local government, responsible for the effective operation of electric and water facilities, was not made subject to the direction of the city manager by the proposed charter revision, he aligned himself with the opponents to the revision.

A great deal of vitriolic discussion ensued and the community was divided about the merits of the proposed change. Indeed, there was formulated a charter revision opposition group which Casper Grathwohl, the former City Attorney, cochaired. I was not politically involved in the affairs of the community and do not recall I felt any urgency to intervene one way or the other.

To the credit of the public relations committee of the charter revision group, it was proposed that a public debate be scheduled in the nature of a Lincoln-Douglas encounter, between an advocate of the City Manager form of government and an advocate of the old weak mayor-council form, such as Niles possessed. Originally Casper Grathwohl, because he was the former City Attorney and cochairman of the group opposing the new form, was requested to meet Harold Klute in public debate. Grathwohl declined the bid because of the pressure of other affairs and suggested that I take and debate the negative of the issue.

I tentatively rejected the invitation for I was nonplused by it. On reflection, I agreed to undertake the debate on an "exploratory basis" with the objective of bringing out both the meritorious as well as the objectionable features of the new charter plan. I pointed out that I was not in any way, officially or informally, associated with the charter opposition group. Mr. Klute quickly responded he was agreeable to the approach and the debate was scheduled to take place in advance of the public vote on January 24, 1955.

Newspaper coverage and radio media publicized the debate held on the stage of the old Niles High School and there assembled on the night of the debate a huge crowd of approximately 1,200 or more interested citizens and their families to hear two attorneys debate an issue shortly to be voted upon.

Harold Klute had well prepared his script and he came on armed with facts, statistics, experiences of other communities, all designed to overwhelm the opposition and garner support for the revision. I recall on the stage feeling I was confronted by a very able advocate presenting with careful analysis a very impressive brief to an appellate court. The court in fact was the men and women who were going to vote on the revision January 24.

I had made but sketchy notes to be the guide for my remarks and I remember standing forward when Harold had finished, expressing some frustration with the way my scribbled notes presented themselves to me, finally tearing them up and lunging into an extemporaneous but enthusiastic defense of the weak mayor council system which had in fact produced strong-willed, capable, civic-minded men to take up the yoke of mayor and, without thought of recompense for personal sacrifice, devote themselves to the promotion of the best interests of the city. I cited then-present Mayor Jerome Wood, a competent industrialist, Dr. Ames and Dr. Fred Bonine, the latter a legendary eye physician of an earlier era, who reputedly served more patients in a day than any physician in the country, some 1,000 a day. I pointed with pride to the Department of Public Works, which was the pride of the city, and the competent Board of Public Safety which managed the Police and Fire Departments and urged that these competent facilities were chaired and made up by local citizens without the requirement of professionally retained personnel to determine our destinies. There was loud applause by the audience.

I will always remember one set of eyes in the front row. Russ Thomas' attention was riveted on me. He was a local restauranteur who had had no particular interest in city government but he was shortly thereafter to seek office as Mayor of Niles and told me later I had inspired him to seek that position. His mayoralty was marked by a vigorous no-nonsense approach to public affairs and it was his administration in the late '50's that carried through over heavy opposition the condemnation of the north half of the block encompassed by Second and Third Streets on the east and west and Main and Sycamore Streets on the north and south, and to construct a modern public parking facility and public restrooms, with access from both Second and Third Streets. Russ Thomas' contributions were memorialized at his death by the erection to his memory of the Thomas Stadium on 11th Street in Niles.

The charter revision went down in defeat when voted on. Harold Klute was always to accuse me of setting Niles back 50 years. Regardless, Niles had the distinction for many years, some would say dubious, of having the only weak mayor council form of government in Michigan. In the process I had secured recognition—some would say notoriety— that no advertisement could have accorded my practice.

SUING THE ONLY BANK IN TOWN

In the late '40's and early '50's, I was being asked to represent substantially more clients from the north end of the county in the vicinity of St. Joseph, the county seat. I was attracting clientele for many miles distant Niles. A reputation for vigorously defending accused persons and advancing actions for personal injuries was perceived, and as a solo practitioner with no insurance or corporate retainers to conflict I was a free unfettered spirit.

One of those early cases had demonstrated that spirit. I sued my bank, the First National Bank of Niles (predecessor of the Old Kent State Bank), something no attorney before or since has done anywhere around in Southwestern Michigan.

The facts were intriguing. In the mid '40's, a little Salvation Army lass came to me with a tale of singular woe. The bank was threatening her with an arrest unless she returned $500 which it claimed she had received in fraud of the bank.

She told me the following: Her son was a veteran of the Iwajima landing in the South Pacific and he had sent her $1,000 of his army pay and asked her to deposit the sum in the bank and save it for him when he returned. The mother did not trust banks. She had lost monies in the closure of the banks in the 1930's, and the experience had not left her any confidence in the banking system. She carried her monies in her purse and she was never far removed from her funds. She opened an account in her name with the First National Bank and her first deposit was the $1,000 sent her by her son. The young teller returned the passbook showing an initial deposit of $1,000 and a balance of $1,000. Remaining at the cage, the mother pondered. If it was good enough for her son it ought to be good enough for her. She pulled out $1,000 of her own money from the bodice of her dress where she carried it and gave it to the teller for inclusion in the initial deposit. The passbook came back with entries on the first line raised from $1,000 to $2,000 for both the deposit and the balance. She was later to make additional deposits and withdrawals which were all reflected and the balance carried forward in the passbook.

There finally came a day about a year and a half later when the balance was reduced to $1,000. With her passbook she went to the bank and withdrew $500, reducing the balance to the sum of $500. That same afternoon, she related to me, the bank called to advise she had overdrawn her account by $500 and she must return the money. She protested she still had $500 in the account. She was asked to bring in her passbook. The bank took possession of the passbook and submitted it to the state crime laboratories for examination. It was reported that the opening entry and the balance figure of the initial entry had been raised from $1,000 to $2,000. Indeed the report had suggested the raising had been done with blue over black ink. The bank threatened her with an arrest for a felony fraud unless the $500 was properly restored to the bank.

The woman was tearful and in obvious distress. She feared arrest but she insisted the monies were hers, or her son's, and there was still $500 in the account. She observed her mistrust in banks generally was proven by the incident. In short she was no self-confessed thief. I was understandably perplexed. The woman was insistent she was telling the truth. An attorney has no right to judge a client, however implausible a story. It is his duty, if he takes a case, to carefully, thoroughly and vigorously prosecute it to such conclusion as he is able, no matter how weak, improbable or uncertain of good result it might appear to another, or to the adverse counsel. There are always two sides to a case and it not infrequently happens that the apparently weaker side wins and the stronger position for some reason fails. That is the challenge of the law. The lawyer who selects, chooses and picks only the strong case—a sure winner—is not really an advocate who would test his mettle in the crucible of the court and jury battle to establish the true merit of the cause. Indeed it is a challenge and a proud one to be able to win an apparently weak case. No case is without some weakness or failure.

I confronted the woman with the following advice which I conceived would test her verity and quickly dispose of the cause on a consultation basis. Yes, the easy and probably most economically sensible way out of the quandary was to return the money to the bank, for in this way she would forego criminal prosecution in the Federal Court in Grand Rapids, which would cost her attorney fees of at least $500, even if she won. If on the other hand she lost, and there was no way of guaranteeing that she would not, she would be a convicted felon and have lost a great deal more. She listened to me in obvious distress. There was another route I explained. I had no conviction she would follow it. She could sue the bank for the remaining $500 she claimed was still in the account!

The woman unhesitatingly said she wished to go that way. Now my feet were in the fire. The First National Bank was my personal bank. It was the only bank in town and it influenced a great deal of power. My office checking account and my personal savings and checking accounts were with the bank. I was well acquainted with its officers, Pat Farguahr, an admirable business-minded Scotsman, and Tom Cain, Sr., the President whose crippled son, Tom Cain, Jr. was a lawyer and Municipal Judge of Niles. I conceived there to be no personal conflict of interest which would have barred my suing the bank, but there remained the strong probability that my entry into litigation with the bank would engender a long period of hostility, hardly conducive to any rapport with the institution in the event specifically I wished to negotiate any loan. In short, there were a host of reasons why I should not hazard the case, not the least being the small amount of money involved and the likelihood of little fee. I believe I had proposed a one-third contingency fee. Even in that day such a case did not promise good financial return for the lawyer.

The die was cast. I promptly filed suit against First National Bank in the Berrien County Circuit Court in St. Joseph. The criminal proceedings against the woman were necessarily aborted. The community buzzed, other lawyers shook their heads and mumbled. One of them, Edwin Donahue, a distinguished trial lawyer, glumly applauded my guts but withheld any critique of my mental approaches. The bank officials were visibly disturbed. No one talked to me and I suppose I did not try very hard to say anything to anyone of the matter. I had the feeling I was removed from polite society. The bank's attorney, Stuart B. White, entered his appearance and his answers starkly portrayed the triable issue, to wit: The bank had been defrauded of $500 owed by my client and they owed her nothing.

I demanded a jury trial and had my first opportunity to test myself on a Circuit Court level with this master at the bar. I had met Attorney White in the Justice of the Peace arena and knew his mettle. Stuart White had a distinguished career as a trial lawyer and in Southwestern Michigan he was recognized as one of the preeminently most capable, vigorous and effective trial lawyers in the area and on par with the best in the state. He was small of stature but an advocate worthy of the best legal opponents arrayed against him. The bank indeed was well and ably represented and regardless of its shock at being sued, must have entered the fray of the ultimate trial to the jury with every confidence.

The bank's witnesses included the teller, a lovely little girl, the Chairman of the Board, Patric Farguahr, and its President, William Cain, Sr., along with Crime Laboratory personnel, the cashier, and the bank accountant. Their testimony was marshaled against one lonely little woman, my client. It must have seemed to the jury a very unequal contest. My examination of the Chairman and the President of the bank attempted a friendly tone. I addressed Mr. Farguahr as "Pat" and Mr. Cain as "Tom." They were rigid in response but not unfriendly. The teller was positive the initial total deposit was $1,000. The cashier observed that if in fact $2,000 had been received in the initial deposit, the young teller's cage that day would have been $1,000 short. My thrust in the cross-examination and my objective was the assertion, which the bank officials could not deny, regardless how they equivocated, that the bank and all of its employees were subject to the human frailty of error and mistake. I used the homely pencil with its eraser attached, the latter to erase mistakes made, and they admitted that there could have been error though it was highly improbable.

My client related she was a Salvation Army lass who collected Christmas pails and worked for the Salvation Army throughout the year at its thrift shop.

The case was not long in presentation. The facts were simple and uncomplicated. The issue was clear. The case really ceased being a civil action. It had turned on the issue "Was my client a thief?"

Stuart White's summation to the jury sounded like the Sermon On the Mount: *THOU SHALT NOT STEAL.* She was an unrepentant thief who had committed the Cardinal Sin and the jury should make short shrift of her. Her sin was worse than theft, for implicit in it was the suggestion the lovely little teller had shorted her cage and embezzled $1,000 from her bank employer. This little woman, parading as a righteous Salvation Army lass, probably routinely dipped her hand into the Christmas pails and rifled through the charitable contributions for clothing and other articles to salvage whatever she wished for her personal use. Referring to my examination of Mr. Cain and Mr. Farguahr, he scathingly upbraided me for familiarly addressing these eminent gentlemen as "Tommy Wommy" and "Patty Watty." Stuart, reaching his full height of 5 feet 5 inches, really laid it on. I had to jump into the fray and literally come out fighting mad.

I did. Banks were human institutions capable of all of the frailties of common men and women. They used, like the rest of us, pencils to erase their errors in the manner of ordinary people. Attorney White had resented my approaching the august persons of the Chairman of the Board and the President of the bank on a level of familiarity, but these individuals were human beings capable of error. The bank operation was not a sacrosanct one beyond criticism. The depositors who entrusted their money to these human institutions with their millions, were not to be treated as subservient vassals dominated by an all-wise, all-dominant master.

The Plaintiff assuredly, if she were in fact a thief, would have given back the money and put a cap on the whole affair. She was putting herself on the line bringing this case before the jury, for if she lost, she was subject surely to criminal prosecution and punishment. I dared the jury to look at the frail, small forlorn looking woman and by their verdict tell me that my client was a wicked, unrepentant thief. This was a careless bookkeeping error by the bank and it should pay its depositor her balance!

The jury retired and was out on deliberation for many hours. The attorneys retired to Niles some 25 miles distant from the Courthouse and awaited the result. I was in my office with clients when the call came from Stuart. He immediately came up to my office and congratulated me openly. We had won and my client was acquitted of the crime of theft. The judgment was for the Plaintiff $500 against the bank.

The conduct of Stuart White in congratulating me on the win was typical of the Niles Bar. The loser always congratulated the winner and no enmities were endured. I always felt the approach was a wholesome one, which much complimented and maintained the morale and esprit of the local bar. Not so Patrick Farguahr, the bank Chairman. He never forgave me for what he claimed was an assault on the bank's integrity.

In the '40's, I was involved in another case involving the first National Bank and specifically Patrick Farguahr as Chairman of the

Board. A young stamp and coin collector had been arrested at the Mission Rock location on the outskirts of Niles at midnight one day along with the local manager of the Michigan Gas Company. A bizarre episode broke which shook the community.

The young man, who I shall refer to as "Ben", aspired to gaining a corner on the 1898 Sesquicentennial World's Fair commemorative postage stamp, of which he already had a goodly number. He had a fine collection of stamps and coins including two complete gold coin sets. He wished to attend an upcoming stamp and coin convention and show of some kind where he anticipated the commemorative stamps would be available and he needed $2,000 cash to attend the show. He had approached the First National Bank and confronted Patrick Farguahr for loan of such amount, offering to put up as collateral his entire collection of stamps and coins, including the gold coins. He stated his purpose for the loan and Mr. Farguahr's response was a short and assertive rejection. The purpose of the loan was inane and the bank would have no part in it.

The young man was not only disappointed, he was bitter and angry that the bank and its Chairman should take such a position. As he glumly pondered his problem of going to the convention emptyhanded and unable to purchase the coveted stamps, he concocted a wild, wholly unreal and indeed a puerile and psychotic scheme to secure his money. He wrote and mailed an anonymous note to Patrick Farguahr, threatening that unless there was deposited in a plain envelope the sum of $2,000 behind the Mission Rock and left there available for him at midnight on a certain day, the Farguahr daughter would be kidnapped and held ransom! The scheme was patently shot with an unreal risk for the quick identification of the sender of the letter but certainly it must have posed for Farguahr a sense of urgency for the safety of his daughter from this spurned loan applicant.

Ben waited and as the day approached for the "drop", his excitement overcame his reason and he spent most of the day drinking in a local bar where he was joined by the manager of the local gas company. It is bizarre what two drinking companions in their cups can conjure, plan and concoct. At the point of intoxication for both of them, Ben mysteriously revealed to the manager that at midnight he was going out to the Mission Rock and he was certain there would be an envelope with $2,000 in it waiting for him. The manager, his brain probably also addled by too much intoxicants, halfheartedly ridiculed the story but was sufficiently intrigued and encouraged to join Ben in going out to the Mission Rock at midnight to recover the cached money. The two of them were at the Rock at midnight when flood lights came on and police apprehended both.

Federal charges were placed against both of them by the District Attorney's office in Grand Rapids. The First National Bank had a national charter and a federal crime was involved, namely the threat to a national bank to extort money. The case against the manager was shortly to be dismissed for he obviously was an unwitting pawn. Ben however confronted a very serious federal charge which could land him in prison.

He asked for my assistance, probably because he didn't have the wherewithal to retain a more prominent attorney. Actually he had no assets other than his stamp and coin collection. He was obviously guilty of a serious crime, and I recognized no defense could be seriously mounted. Here was a very foolish young man who had permitted his emotions to control reason and impulsively commit a bizarre, possibly temporarily deranged act. The only prospect I would envision was to plead him guilty and move for probation or leniency in the light of his prior good record.

I questioned the value of his gold coin collection. Each set had coins variously dated in excellent condition in denominations of two twenty dollars, two ten dollars, two five dollars, two $2.50 and one $1 coins. Each set had a face value of $76 with a market value at $300. I agreed to take one set for my fee and gave him a receipt for $300 fees. Today the set would be worth $3,000.

I presented Ben to the Federal Court in Grand Rapids on a plea of guilty and made an impassioned plea for leniency on the basis of a good, prior record and his youthful incapacity to confront the bank rejection of his loan application. He had an overbroad commitment to preserve in one collection the entire 1898 Sesquicentennial commemorative stamp, which only an ardent collector could understand. Happily, probation was granted, and a bizarre incident in this young man's life fortuitously did not terminate in the disaster of a prison record.

PEOPLE VS. KATHY WATSON

In the early '40's a sensational criminal extortion case surfaced in Niles and was tentatively offered me to represent. Both circumstances and my gut instinct caused me to decline.

Kathryn Watson was a large, brassy, much bejeweled woman approximately 45 or more years old, who had come recently into the community of Niles from Chicago with her ex-husband, a Chicago policeman. She had been arrested and posted bond on a charge of extortion for approximately $3,500 from a local jeweler, one Ray Chappel. They sought my services and counsel and she told me that any monies she had received from the jeweler was for jewelry, rings and gold she had at different times sold to him.

The whole story did not sound right to me and while I was sorting out her statements, she suddenly said she very much wanted me to be associated in her case with an older more experienced lawyer. She wished to retain Stuart White as co-counsel. My position was that while I had the greatest respect for Stuart White, she did not need two lawyers to represent her and I indicated I would bow out of the picture.

Stuart White was to call me shortly and advise that he had called his very good friend, Kim Sigler, one of Michigan's most eminent trial lawyers, whose offices were in Lansing, Michigan, and that the latter had agreed to take on the case. Stuart White asked me to stay with the case and assist Sigler. His advice was that the experience of an association with Mr. Sigler in the trial of the case would be of significant training benefit to me. He urged me to stay with the case.

Kim Sigler at the time was the most colorful attorney in the state of Michigan. It was said of him that he had over 50 suits, ties, shirts and shoes to match and that in trial he commonly appeared in different outfits during the morning and afternoon sessions. He had a string of court victories and was commonly regarded as the peer model among trial lawyers. Stuart White numbered Sigler among his closest friends. Sigler was later to be elected Governor of the State of Michigan and would have given Stuart any appointment that was available. He offered Stuart an appointment to the Berrien County Circuit court bench when Fremont Evans died, but Mr. White declined and ultimately was to accept appointment to the Chairmanship of the Public Service Commission in Lansing.

That turned out to be a post that Stuart should not have taken for it required travel between Lansing and his home in Niles and an accident enroute home cost Stuart his life.

Stuart's friendly advice that I stay in association with Sigler in the Watson case did persuade me to remain through the preliminary examination before the Justice of Peace proceedings to determine whether there was probable cause to bind Kathryn Watson over to the Circuit Court.

I did not participate in the preliminary examination but I did have occasion to watch Attorney Sigler who awed me and all of the court Personnel. He could have stepped out of a Brooks' Brothers advertisement. He was tall, handsome, erect and impeccably clothed. His presence was arresting. He lent drama and authority to his participation in the examination of the State's witnesses. Mrs. Watson did not testify.

The proofs presented by the witnesses, chiefly the complainant, Ray Chappel, the jeweler, left me personally with no confidence in the client's cause and I felt a sense of relief that I would not be responsible for the defense. Ray Chappel was a married man of some 64 years of age at the time. He had operated for many years a jewelry business in Niles on the Main Street next to the Western Union. He had a workshop and a small darkroom in the rear of his jewelry store where he fitted glasses to customers. He testified that Mrs. Watson had patronized his store several times and on March 21, 1941, she brought him a small case containing some old gold which he took into the back room for examination. She followed him there and the two of them had intercourse. He testified this happened with some frequency and later on or about May 14, 1941, she told him she was pregnant and that he was responsible. He was to testify that she had told him she had had a medical examination in Chicago confirming the pregnancy and was told that an abortion there would cost approximately $400 and that she preferred to have the abortion in South Bend, a short distance removed, and he had given her $5 to get a medical opinion in South Bend. He said that she had reported back to him after she had the examination and was strong enough to undergo the abortion operation which was criminal, but that she needed $450 for the abortionist. The gullible jeweler, never questioning that this 45 year old married woman was pregnant, went on to relate he fell into the scam and he testified that he paid her the $450 for the criminal operation.

I recall that I sat numbed by the testimony that spilled from this wretchedly gullible and foolish man and more and more wanted to distance myself from the case. He was to relate that the Defendant plied him thereafter with a rapid succession of notes and pleas sent by various messengers describing her desperate and dangerous condition the result of the criminal abortion, for which she blamed him. He went on to say that he would pay the messenger at short intervals various sums of money which in a short time totaled over $3,000. Mr. Chappel was to testify that on August 29, 1941, he received two notes from the Defendant, the one complaining that she had developed a very serious condition, could not tell her husband about it, and she asked him for a large sum of money and a quick response within the hour. In that same hour a second and more threatening note was received by him from the messenger and was introduced into the evidence of the case. That note read as follows:

"Do you want me to go to the county house for this treatment? I am ready to air the whole thing—as I am doing the suffering—not you. If you don't—what other course have I—as if it wasn't for you I could tell him all, as I don't care for myself. If you do not reply to this I will send for him to come here and bring an attorney with him as I can't go on like this. You must know this is terrible. I can't help the condition—as you made me get rid of same—you paid for it— and left me in this condition.

Now think this over Ray dear—I am sorry but am sick and just can't help it. Please reply."

Mr. Chappel testified he consulted counsel who notified the sheriff who in turn arranged for a deputy to wait in the dark back room. On September 4, 1941, a female messenger showed and asked for the package for the Defendant. She was arrested and led the deputy to the Defendant who was waiting around the corner in a big black sedan. The Defendant then and there was arrested.

Mrs. Watson, to my embarrassment, turned out to be an unscrupulous, scheming blackmailer. I told Kim Sigler I could not continue to associate myself in the case. He obviously didn't need me. I was of no value in the case. The case was lost and I believed it had to be lost. If it was somehow won, I certainly would get no credit. Kim Sigler had the idea that the prosecution would not be able to present a *prima facie* case of extortion. He was to urge at the Circuit Court trial that the Defendant's threat to publicly accuse Chappel did not rise to the level of a public accusation of a crime such as would be involved if the Defendant had threatened to file a formal complaint and instigate criminal prosecution. It was a technical defense for which I had no sympathy. I withdrew from the case.

Kathryn Watson was bound over to Circuit Court for the trial and Kim Sigler alone handled the defense. She never took the stand to testify and Sigler's motion to Circuit Court Judge Fremont Evans to dismiss the prosecution and direct a verdict not guilty on the grounds that a *prima facie* case of extortion was not presented, was denied, and the Defendant was found guilty. Sigler's appeal to the Supreme Court of Michigan failed to overturn the verdict (People vs. Watson, 307 Mich 378).

At the time of the trial the community buzzed with the news. Chappel had admitted having other clandestine affairs with female customers of his store. He was commonly and demeaningly referred to as "Raping Ray Chappel." His store became an anathema in the community and women feared to patronize him. The rear room took on an ominous nature. Ray Chappel was shortly to cease doing business. As for Mrs. Watson it must be assumed that she had used the ploy or scam with some frequency before she laid the net for "Raping Ray." Her husband must have been in on the scam. The female messenger ploy who carried the demand notes, must also have been part of a well-oiled conspiracy employed in similar manner at various times and places.

MARY'S ISRAELITE CITY OF DAVID - WAS QUEEN MARY MORTAL AFTER ALL?

In the early '50's a new and novel National Lawyer's Association was initially formed which was to greatly affect the lives and practice of trial lawyers throughout the country. The National Association of Compensation Claimants Attorneys operating under the acronym NACCA was the result of a few attorneys, including its first president, Ben Marcus of Muskegon, Michigan, meeting in Portland, Oregon. Primarily involving workmen's compensation counsel, they were also interested in general tort and personal injury litigation. The National Association quickly attracted the attention and membership of many lawyers who wished to advance their skills in the personal injury field and had no other forum, seminars or schools to address for training. I joined the group early because I believed the seminars and teaching facilities were what plaintiffs' attorneys needed.

The moot law courts of the law schools of the era provided little background for the attorney interested in trial strategy. Down the pike there loomed a whole new host of trial frontiers in damages, torts, automobile litigation, construction site accidents, products liability, governmental immunity cases and ultimately malpractice actions. The new association later to be renamed the American Trial Lawyers Association (ATLA) was to provide the interchange between trial lawyers of their teaching skills and experiences in these areas which promised new and extended frontiers of the law. I was determined to mount and be at the forefront of some of those frontiers.

I began doing a very wide range of practice in criminal and tort actions and clients came to me a considerable distance removed from the small town of Niles and predominantly from the north end of Berrien County.

One Sunday afternoon in the summer of 1954, three persons having arranged an appointment with me at my summer residence on Lake Michigan in St. Joseph, introduced themselves to me as Coy S. Purnell, Betty Purnell Marks and Lucille Purnell Lunt. They were the grandchildren of "King Ben and Queen Mary Purnell," the titular heads of the City of David religious colony in St. Joseph, Michigan.

Those two had started life together, virtually penniless, traveling from town to town preaching a new cultist faith ascribing to Ben the powers of a seventh messenger of God. Over the years they gathered a large following and they brought their believing flock at the turn of the century to Benton Harbor and started the Israelite Colony of the House of David. The colony grew, prospered and became famous around the world, and was noted especially for its traveling bearded, long-haired baseball teams.

In 1927-28, sensational criminal charges of immorality were made against Benjamin involving ritualistic sexual affairs with female members who were kept apart from the males. A Grand Jury investigation on a State lawsuit for receivership was fought all the way to the Michigan Supreme Court in 1928. Benjamin, old and broken, died in 1927 and a deep factional fight erupted between Mary, who always defended

Benjamin's innocence, and Attorney H.T. Dewhurst, who succeeded to the cult leadership. Mary considered Dewhurst a scheming unscrupulous traitor and she and her followers withdrew and founded a cult of her own. The Court Decree split up the assets between the original House of David and Mary's offshoot which became known as Mary's Israelite City of David.

Mary and Ben had only one son, S. Coy Purnell, who survived them. The three young people I was interviewing were Coy S. (or Sam) Purnell, Heddy Marks and Lucy Lunt, and they were the children of S. Coy Purnell. They were King Ben and Queen Mary's only grandchildren. In effect, they were the only legal lineal heirs of Mary Purnell and the latter's death in August 1952 placed them in a position to claim their inherited shares of her estate.

Mary Purnell had participated in a Trust Agreement approximately 1952 at the age of 90 years and she had abdicated her throne of administrative leadership over the colony in favor of a board of four trustees of which she remained one, with the colony the sole beneficiary. She continued her role as spiritual leader until her death in 1953. Her word was undisputed law in the colony. She had decreed that her grandson, Coy, live rent free in a colony residence and regardless of the adverse litigation which we were about to commence, the members of the colony never disputed that decision.

Not one of the three grandchildren or the families were members of Mary's cult. Indeed the cult had shrunk to about 160 members, because no new converts were being attracted and marriage between males and females was forbidden. Marriage was considered a worldly pleasure to be eschewed. Most of the remaining members were past 50 years of age and there were few young people among them. The colony had assets approximating $750,000, of which at least $300,000, oddly enough all in real estate, was recorded in the name alone of Mary Purnell. This real estate was widely spread and consisted of many homes, lots, and farms in various places as far removed as Australia.

Mary Purnell had taught her followers, and they believed, that she was pure and sinless and since the wages of sin was death, she would never die. She was a peer model for her followers.

It was odd that $300,000 in value of real estate was recorded in the name alone of Mary Purnell individually and in no sense as trustee for the colony. Any convert or follower of the cult upon entering the cult had to divest himself of his property, for it was contrary to the cult's religious belief for a member to own property. Mary's cult as well as the original House of David taught that property ownership begets sin. The members surrendered their property and pledged all earnings in the future to the colony upon entering the cult.

Coy went on to tell me, and this later was proven true, that attorneys for the cult urged and advised that the property recorded in Mary's name individually be designated as trust property so that in the event of the "unlikely death" of Mary, there would be no contest. The cultists had responded negatively to the advice. Queen Mary was pure, sinless and truly immaculate. She had taught that death was the wages of sin and evil. She was purity incarnate, inviolable, and would forever live. More than that, being a pure model, if her followers were believers and sinless, they too would enjoy immortality. The unconditional surrender to her of all right, title and possession of those parcels registered in her name alone was a testimonial of their faith. It was not brought about by any inadvertency or carelessness on the part of anyone registering the title.

So strong was that faith that when Mary Purnell drew her last breath on August 19, 1952, at the ripe old age of 91, rumor had it that she was buried upright, for the cultists refused to believe she was long departed and believed instead that she would rise again and be with them. They were making it easy for her to depart the grave! Her residence quarters in the colony were kept and regularly maintained in scrupulously clean condition. Her clothes were hung and the bed was made daily for many years. The cultists refused to believe that she was other than temporarily removed and their faith would not have it otherwise.

This in brief was the background presented me. Coy Jr. was to tell me he loved his grandmother and she responded. All he asked was to secure for himself and his sisters a rightful inheritance to those properties titled in her separate and individual name.

I was astonished but intrigued. These young people were in fact Mary Purnell's only lineal heirs and entitled to inherit her estate if there in fact was an estate. My advice was to file a petition for probate of her estate and ask for appointment of the grandson, Coy Purnell, as sole administrator. Coy agreed and there was to follow one of the most bizarre and colorful cases of my trial career, withal it did not terminate in a jury trial. As long as it lasted it was Page One news grist and there is no doubt it greatly boosted my trial reputation.

When the petition seeking Coy's appointment for the deceased, Mary Purnell, was filed, its publication literally exploded a veritable storm wind of controversy in Benton Harbor. Full-page, large black lettered headlines, CULTISTS SHOCK—DENY HEIRS CLAIM. News reporting for many days explored and reviewed the history of the sect. There were many interviewed and reported individual reactions of the cultists to the probate proceedings, which in effect denied them their fundamentalist belief in Mary's immortality. Lawyers for the cult and I for the heirs made long statements to the press. It was as though the whole community was being played to as a vast jury. Long before the day of universal television, the press so thoroughly covered the news, it is now hard to believe that any panel of 12, disinterested, impartial, unknowing jurors could have been selected on the occasion of ultimate jury trial. The cultists were reported to be shocked that Queen Mary's blood grandchildren were claiming a large share of their property, but they "put their faith in God." They were reported to be visibly under an emotional strain and stress. One of them, a little spry woman named Lizzie, said, "Brother Benjamin told us the day would come when we would be down to two cents and sorely tried. The Bible teaches you must be tried and this is our trial." The case for the heirs was taking on the trappings of a Satan designed to harass, test and bedevil the colony. Attorney Humphrey Gray who had been counsel for the cult since 1935 made a statement shrugging off the probate proceedings saying that whatever property remained in Mary Purnell's name at the time of her death was there by inadvertence and that all property bought, improved, and maintained, was from trust monies. He said in one newspaper accounting that someone obviously must have been careless in taking title in her name rather than in the trust. In truth, he said, "It was contrary to the religious beliefs for any member, including Mary, to own property, for property ownership begets sin."

This was the position taken by the Gray lawfirm. No opposition was presented in the probate petition and appointment of the administrator. A Circuit Court injunctive proceedings however was shortly filed against the administrator and the three children in the Berrien County Circuit Court to restrain Coy from proceeding further and the battle lines were drawn by our answer in Circuit Court which alleged that Mary Purnell was not, in the accepted sense, a member of the colony or bound by its rules and regulations relative to the ownership of property. Our answer went on to throw down the gauntlet. It alleged:"At all times, her right to own and hold title to property was recognized by both officers and members of the colony."

If we were the agents of Satan to test the colony to its core as the members now putting on sack cloth and ashes were complaining, we would be bold about it. Michigan's "Dead Man's Statute" required that the lips of the deceased being sealed, any adverse claimant against the estate was also silenced. I was to argue that the colony and the cultists were adverse claimants against the estate of Mary Purnell and since they had an interest in the cause, neither they nor their attorneys could controvert or dispute Mary's title to the properties in her name alone titled.

It was a thin but vital thread upon which to hang. We took the position on effect that the grandson, Coy Jr., now the administrator of the estate of Mary Purnell, Deceased, was the only one privileged to speak for the Queen. The cult followers were adverse claimants against her estate!

Humphrey Gray, then in his 70's, had brought into his firm a young attorney, John Globensky, to replace his son, Luman Gray, who had died several years prior, cutting short a promising law career. John was a fine student of the law having graduated at the top of his class at Notre Dame Law School. This was among John's first, if not indeed first, legal effort. There was no question the firm could not use cult members, officers or attorneys to establish that the Queen held in trust the property titled in her name, individually, without violating the Dead Man's Statute. Globensky set in motion a search for a disenchanted cultist, who had left the sect but was close enough to the facts to responsively testify, if such were the case, that Mary Purnell actually was trustee of such property for the colonists and had no personal right or interest in the property titled in her name. His search turned up a former secretary to the Queen, a devoted friend and confidante for many years who had become disaffected of the sect, had left the community and was living in Houston, Texas. It turned out that she had simply joined another cult known as the "Great I Am" sect.

Globensky scheduled the deposition of the former secretary at the Shamrock Hotel in Houston, Texas in the early part of 1955. The witness confirmed, unshaken by my critical cross-examination, that it was intended by all that Mary Purnell take title to the questioned property for the sole benefit of the colonists and she had joined in that intent. Since the woman had no interest in the affairs of the City of David colony, her testimony, critically conclusive of our position, passed the muster of objection.

I was to tell Coy Jr. that the former secretary's testimony doomed our position and he should settle as best he could his action with the colony. No settlement was ever offered or gained by him. The colonists alone agreed, pursuant to Queen Mary's order, regardless of his pursuit of the legal action against them, he and his family would have lifetime free tenancy of his residence at the colony.

I had always known our case must founder if the defense found an impartial witness outside the cult. The venture however was a dramatic and rewarding experience. I had shaken some rafters in the Benton Harbor area.

THE BENTON HARBOR FIRE DEPARTMENT SCANDALS

A sensational trial in Berrien Circuit Court took place in 1952 which was to cause the disruption of the Benton Harbor Fire Department, the ouster of its Chief, and political reverberations for years. The Bertha Russell vs. Ray Hall case had its ominous beginnings for the Chief and the Fire Department with the dismissal of a fireman. The drama ran its course inexorably, like a Greek tragedy.

In August, 1952, First Class Fireman Louis T. Miller sought out my help to contest his ouster from the Department August 5, 1952. He had been summarily fired by the Chief for "conduct unbecoming a city employee," obviously a loose label. Miller complained that morale was low in the Department because of nepotism and favoritism practiced by the Chief in the promotion of personnel. The Chief's son, a fireman, was favored for promotion, despite seniority of others. There was an under-current of malaise involving a well known local madame which was riddling the Department's esprit and endangering the effectiveness of an agency entrusted with a vital aspect of public safety.

50

I had always taken the position that I would without recompense *pro bono* represent any policeman or fireman who sought my services in a worthy cause. I agreed on Miller's behalf to call for a Civil Service Board hearing at the Benton Harbor City Hall to inquire the justification of his ouster and demand reinstatement.

I proposed to fully air the Department row and I sent off a letter to the City Manager, Pat Crow, advising we were going to contest the Chief's ouster of Miller for alleged misconduct and that I proposed to call fellow firemen to testify in his defense to the low morale in the department under the Chief's autocratic control. Additionally, I would call as a witness Bertha Russell who, for many years, had openly operated a house of prostitution in Benton Harbor. My listing of her was certain to transmit tremors of apprehension to the authorities that I would explore the Department's problems to the hilt. I asked for subpoenas for the City Clerk, an ex-fireman who had been discharged, and six firemen, including the Assistant Chief. I was signaling the City Manager who had been a top rank reserve naval officer, my determination that the hearing be no whitewash.

The scheduled hearing not only promised, it did not fail to produce the stormiest, most unusual and explosive session in the history of the three-member Civil Service Board. My request for the subpoenas addressed to City Hall broke like a bomb and the *News Palladium*, the local newspaper, began to put out large black print headlined front-paged stories, "FIRE DEPARTMENT ROW TO BE AIRED, ACCUSATIONS FLY, MANAGER WILL PROBE BENTON HARBOR FIRE DEPARTMENT MESS," and others, which covered the front pages like a continuing war story. These releases continued for a month after the hearing, covering many sequel stories.

At the hearing City Attorney W.H. Cunningham promptly asked and the Board acquiesced that testimony be limited to what he said would be "strictly pertinent" to the Miller ouster. It immediately became obvious that a whitewash was developing. I was denied the opportunity to introduce testimony of Madame Russell which would have exposed the corruption that riddled the department.

She was however to remain in the wings, though I did not know it at the time, waiting to step forward in her own case against Hall. Six fellow officers were ready and willing to respond to their subpoenas under the protection of which, they testified that Miller was a good, conscientious, able and very studious fireman deserving promotion. They testified further there was a system of 'palace favorites' in the department fostered by the Chief, under which only a favored few could possibly hope to advance in rank. One of these was the Chief's son. There was the general feeling among the men that promotion examinations were irregular. Low morale and a great deal of tension, destructive of discipline, was the result.

Miller testified that he had been the President of the Local International Association of Firemen (AFL), which represented the firemen in wage negotiations with the City. He was a World War II combat veteran and had been with the fire department since 1946. His fellow firemen attested he was the most studious, well versed, conscientious man in the department, and they denied he was ever guilty of insubordination.

Hall was to testify Miller was a radical who complained the examinations were rigged and that he had dismissed him because he was a nuisance. But other testimony drew attention to the circumstance that Miller actually was fired the same night he had approached the Chief's son and told the latter that his fellow officers were cold-shouldering him because it was expected he would shortly be advanced in rank over other more deserving and more senior members in rank and that this was generally resented.

The Board recessed to deliberate its findings and determination, after I had summarized a call for justice for Miller and a restoration of discipline and morale to the department. I was told there would be no decision short of three weeks.

Events shortly occurred which greatly exacerbated the crisis and focused attention to the problems of the fire department. Chief Hall summarily discharged one of the firemen who had testified for Miller. Another fireman who had testified was discharged shortly thereafter, but he was restored to his post just as summarily by the City Manager, who then in turn suspended the Chief and announced that there would be a formal investigation of the department in an attempt to restore order, discipline and morale. It shortly began to appear that whether or not the Civil Service Board ever got around to being motivated by the testimony and charges to objectively make a determination of the charges brought out in the hearing, the City authorities were moving to a solution long overdue. Chief Hall did not remain quiet. He publicly accused an ex-city commissioner who had made some derogatory remarks of trying to smear and discredit him. The city fathers were indeed confronted by a crisis in the department which now threatened to blow wide open.

Nothing which had occurred however was to match the intensely emotional, sheer suspense and public-gripped drama of the event, which, within a week of the hearing, was to overpower and render pale all else which had gone before.

THE CASE OF MADAME BERTHA RUSSELL

The woman in red emerged from the shadows and sought my assistance. Bertha Russell had for years been recognized as the Madam of Benton Harbor. She was a woman in her 50's who had long been in prostitution. She appeared to have been well regarded in many high placed circles as a woman who, regardless of her seamy profession, was charitable to a fault and possessed of redeeming characteristics which earned her some grudging admiration by many in the community. It was said of her that on one occasion when Governor Dickinson rode in the leading parade car in a Blossomland Parade through the streets of Benton Harbor, he rode unwittingly in Bertha's white Cadillac, a circumstance which would have totally discomfited the staid, puritan-minded Governor, if he had known. Bertha's acts of charity were legion, as were her defenders and she was a prominent established fixture in Benton Harbor in the '40's and '50's.

I had asked her to come forward in the Miller case because I knew she could finger corruption if it existed in the department. Denied that avenue by the Commission's early ruling, there remained only hints of the corruption which sorely troubled the department.

Charles Gore, prominent Benton Harbor trial lawyer, had in the past represented her in various matters but he had refused to be involved in the instant case and had suggested she get out-of-town counsel. I was probably handling more Benton Harbor trial matters than most intown counsel, but I qualified as an out-of-towner and my involvement in the Miller case was sufficient to lead Bertha Russell to me.

Bertha was to tell me that she had consorted with Ray Hall for many years and she had provided her girls regularly for various firemen's parties and visiting conventions and get-togethers. She told me that she had loaned the chief three separate amounts totaling $1,133, all without receipts in April of 1949. Two of them served to erect a tombstone over the grave of a marine son killed in the Iwajima assault in World War II. The sum of $233 was given him to cover a fine assessed by the City Manager for, of all things, being seen at Bertha's house, after being repeatedly warned. The receipt for this $233 she told me, and she was later to testify to it in Court, had been given by Hall to her for safekeeping, but it was confiscated by the police in a raid on her house of prostitution in April of 1950. It appeared that Bertha long sustained Hall's association and imposition upon her all in the hope that the two of them would ultimately marry. Her patience was to be shattered when he married instead a retired and very respectable school teacher.

I filed an action in Circuit Court sounding *in Assumpsit*, demanding the payment of the sum of $1,133 all with interest at 5% from April, 1949. The newspaper featured the suit and Chief Hall's reaction: "That woman has never given me a penny and I defy her to prove otherwise," he said. He charged that the suit was just one more step in a smear campaign against him.

The fat was in the fire. The local Circuit Court Judges excused themselves presiding in the case. Hall was unable to secure local counsel and he was to retain Attorney Robert Linsey of Grand Rapids to represent him. Kalamazoo County Circuit Court Judge Lucius Sweet, a very capable and experienced jurist, was appointed to preside. Sweet later, whenever I saw him over a period of many years, was to recall and reflect on the trial as the most exciting he had ever presided over, one so well orchestrated with script as to deserve Hollywood screening.

Bertha Russell was the classic Madame. Ray Hall could not have been better played by any actor than himself.

Bertha was magnificent on the stand. She told how she and Hall had consorted at the Detroit Tuller Hotel in 1949 during a Firemen's Convention, at a Muskegon hotel and at other places, and that Hall frequently visited her in her bedroom in Benton Harbor. There in April 1949, she was to give him on three occasions $200 in partial payment of his deceased son's memorial stone, and later $700 to finish payment of the stone. Critically, it developed in the case, she had given him a third loan of $233 to pay his fine for having been seen at her home by the City Manager after several warnings. No receipts were taken and no witnesses. Hall had given her the receipt of $233 for his fine and this, she said, was confiscated by the police in a raid on her premises. The Benton Harbor Police Chief was subpoenaed and he said he participated in the raid but did not remember seeing the receipt among Bertha's effects. The City Treasurer however tendered a copy of the original receipt for $233 which Bertha identified except for the color, as a duplicate of the one she had received for safekeeping from Hall. One of the police in on the raid said he had seen a receipt among the papers seized among Bertha's effects which was made out to Hall in the amount of $233. The web of circumstantial evidence was being drawn tighter.

One of Bertha's girls testified she brought an envelope from Bertha to Ray Hall on April 15, 1949, the date of the money advanced to him, but she did not know what was in it. A fireman testified he saw the girl give Hall something on that date. A loan company officer testified that on April 21, 1945, when Bertha claimed she had advanced $700 to Hall for the rest of his son's memorial stone, she had borrowed from the loan company $500.

Bertha testified she had to borrow $500 to get enough money to give Chief Hall. When Attorney Linsey, cross-examining Bertha, seeking to discredit her after she related she had for many years operated a house of prostitution, asked her whether or not as a citizen she had ever paid real estate taxes on her property, she responded quickly, calmly and with a demeanor which must have masked her real feelings: "Yes, Mr. Attorney," she said, "I have for years paid my taxes, both in the spring and the fall. The police department regularly raids my establishment. I line up my girls before the judge, he fines each of them and I pay the fines." She had neatly and deftly turned the answer to the question to her advantage.

Ray Hall was a big wheel in firemen's' associations. That year he was chaplain of the National Firemen's Association and President of the Michigan Fire Chief's Association. In the summer of 1954, the state convention of the Firemen's Association was scheduled in Benton Harbor. Bertha testified that Hall had her girls available for entertainment for all visiting firemen.

Hall's testimony that he had never taken a dime from Bertha by gift or loan and that he never consorted with her or frequented hotels or other cities with her in tow, was confounded by the circumstantial proofs relating to the missing City Clerk's receipt for the sum of $233, which I could argue was confiscated from her, probably in a cooperative police raid. His admission that he had received an envelope from one of Bertha's girls at his office was not embellished by the flaky explanation there was no money received, only a note asking his opinion of the advisability, if any, of making a loan to one of his firemen. Finally the testimony of various fire equipment and hose salesmen that they had seen Bertha in out-of-town hotels with him put in stark relief the ultimate argument: who was telling the truth?

Attorney Linsey was to thunder in summation: "Are you going to believe a notorious criminal or are you going to believe a man, highly honored in his profession, who was never arrested or in any trouble until September of last year when he was dismissed from the Benton Harbor Fire Department?" I was to counter with the argument, in no way facetious: "Bertha Russell is an admitted prostitute; she has bared her past. Ray Hall is a perjurer who has only recently been caught up with."

The jury of six men and six women deliberated two hours and returned a verdict of $1,133 plus $212 accumulated interest in favor of Bertha Russell and against the deposed fire chief. The Benton Harbor *News Palladium*, which had followed the entire series of cases involving Hall with four star extras was to publish the next day an editorial:

MORE THAN A DEBT

A circuit court jury late Wednesday wrote another — and it is hoped the last — chapter in the sordid story involving Benton Harbor's dismissed fire chief and an admitted former keeper of a house of prostitution.

Suspended and then discharged from a high city post for misconduct, Ray Hall was found by a court jury to owe a debt of $1,133 to Bertha Russell, who brought suit to force repayment of the loan.

As the trial of the suit unfolded, the jury was confronted by one basic issue: did Hall borrow the money, and did he repay it, or did he not?

Mrs. Russell swore that she did loan the former fire chief the money, at his request. Hall testified under solemn oath that he never asked for nor received a loan.

In the final analysis, and after taking five ballots, the jury reached a decision — it decided that the plaintiff's story was true and that the defendant's denials were not.

The jury, of course, was obliged to weigh all the evidence and to pass judgment upon the veracity of the principles and the witnesses. In applying the measure to Hall, the jurors were considering a man who for several years headed one of the city's most important departments and who bore the responsibility of public trust. Bertha Russell's "profession" was not such as to contribute to society and the community, to say the least.. She certainly could not bring before the jury in open court a moral background. But despite her past, her truthfulness was believed by the jury. Perhaps — we are not prepared to say — it might have been better had she 'written off' the debt. She chose the other course.

Morality is a broad term, covering not only the age-old question of sex, but sincerity, principles and, above all, honesty. At least it can be said for Bertha Russell that she has made no pretenses. This civil action aroused wide public interest because it touched certain fundamentals so clearly dealt with in the greatest Book of all.

The verdict capped a series of reversals for Hall since he had been fired from his job by the Benton Harbor City Manager in September 1954. He had lost an appeal to the City Pension Board in an attempt to save the bulk of a 25-year pension fund which would have been due him later in 1955. He later lost a reinstatement attempt before the City

Civil Service Board. He in effect was a very broken man.

Oddly, he called me personally on the phone shortly after the verdict. I had mixed feelings for I felt that he should have thoroughly hated me. To my surprise he was to tell me that he bore me no rancor. He recognized I was doing my duty by my client and he admired my effort. Then he related he had lost a $40,000 pension and was broke and he wanted me to take over the task for him of recovering his pension rights. I must confess all contempt that I had had for him quickly left me and I wanted to help him. The business of taking from him his pension struck me as being a low blow and I sympathized with his plight. I had a sharp conflict and I told him quickly that he must understand it. I had prominently been identified in the public eye with the proceedings which had brought him low. My jumping to his side would seriously reflect on my integrity. He agreed.

Throughout the trial, my wife Rachel and my 80-year old mother had been in daily attendance, following with rapt attention the unfolding drama. This was no new experience for Rachel for she routinely attended all of my trials and critiqued, applauded or criticized my maneuvers, examinations and summations, to her great credit and my very substantial benefit. Whether she knew it or not, I was really playing my role of trial advocate to the hilt in order to pique her interest. My mother had not had such frequent opportunity to see her son in action and she was elated. I turned to Bertha and said gallantly to her at the trial's end that I should be honored to have her as my guest for dinner in the main dining room of the Whitcomb Hotel in St. Joseph, Michigan, at that time a most prestigious and elegant dining room. Bertha turned to me in amazement: "Young man, you're asking for a lot of embarrassment. Everyone knows me and you would not like to be seen with me, especially at the Whitcomb." I told her that we would have a table reserved in the center of the dining room and my mother and wife would join us. Enroute to the dining room and at the table, Bertha was to regale us with stories of her past. My mother and wife were fascinated with the woman and it was high adventure for both of them. "Why you know," said Bertha, "in my prime, I could walk down the center aisle of any church in Benton Harbor or St. Joseph and looking either way, spot a goodly number of my clients." More important, our presence in the dining room was shortly noted and indeed Bertha was very well known. Charles Gore, a prominent attorney, and Stanley Banyon, publisher of the News Palladium, warmly congratulated Bertha and me on our hard fought victory. It was a heady, unforgettable evening.

THE CASE OF DEMARIA VS. MAYOR FLAUGH

My reputation for taking on politically risky cases, regardless the amount involved must have earned me the next unusual case which I handled in Benton Harbor. Leon DeMaria, owner of the Italian Village Restaurant, a former political ally of Benton Harbor mayor, Joseph Flaugh, was rankled that the mayor had not repaid him a $300 loan which he had given him in 1949 while he was engaged in an unsuccessful bid to unseat former Benton Harbor mayor Leon Gideon.

The mayor had insisted the loan was advanced in fact by a cousin of DeMaria, one Anthony Mendela who had died and he refused to pay the sum to DeMaria. It seemed a small matter at best but there was principle involved and tempers had raised the matter to fever pitch. It became a matter of family pride with DeMaria that Flaugh be compelled to pay the loan by whatever means (*sic*) he could bring against the latter. DeMaria had sought me out and I listened to his impassioned tale. He had served the mayor loyally as a Benton Harbor Fourth Ward political ally and had been responsible for drumming up a great deal of Italian support for Flaugh, who was a popular officeholder. Flaugh had needed $300 but had told DeMaria that he had no security. DeMaria, who frequently got money from his cousin, was advised by the latter that he would not put up the money directly without security, but that he would give it to DeMaria to loan to Flaugh on his own terms. DeMaria said he had repaid the loan to his cousin and Flaugh owed him the money directly. There were no receipts to support his claim.

I opined that the only way to legally force the issue (which should only be legally enforced), was to sue the mayor. I remember DeMaria cocking his head and questioning my sanity. I must be crazy! The mayor was the most powerful Democratic politician and office holder in the area. Why he had even had so much influence in Lansing that he was principally responsible for Attorney Tom Robinson's appointment by the governor to the Berrien County Circuit Court. What chance did I think I would have of getting a fair trial from Circuit Court Judge Robinson? He was clearly pessimistic.

Judge Robinson was one of the very few Democrats of any prominence in Berrien County. He had long established himself as a vigorous and very able trial lawyer in Benton Harbor and he was universally respected and admired for his courage and very competent representation of every cause entrusted to him. I had every confidence that Judge Robinson, no matter his friendship, acquaintance or any political contacts he had had with Flaugh, would be impeccably fair in any trial over which he presided. DeMaria was not content. He warned me that I would take the case at my peril and my career would be prejudiced handling his case against Flaugh in Judge Robinson's court.

There certainly was not a great deal involved. Primarily I resented the suggestion that a Circuit Judge would be other than impartial. I filed the action and advanced the case to jury trial in February of 1954.

On the opening of Court, the room back of the bar was filled with DeMaria clanspeople, at least 75 strong. To my surprise, they all arose in unison, out of respect to DeMaria and myself, when we entered the Courtroom. The Judge's appearance shortly thereafter and the bailiff's admonition to all rise seemed almost to have secondary import.

DeMaria testified from the stand that the mayor had pleaded with him at his home in 1949 that he badly needed money in the campaign and had no collateral . DeMaria had secured the money on loan from his cousin, Anthony Mendela, who had agreed to loan it to DeMaria who then could make the unsecured loan to Flaugh if he wished. DeMaria went on to say he repaid his cousin before he died in 1952. He had a dozen or more times asked the mayor for repayment up until the very day before the suit was commenced, but all to no avail. He was cross-examined by the defense attorney on the matter of receipts and DeMaria responded: "My cousin and I were family. We never gave receipts and I never gave him a note. I borrowed money this way from my cousin for 15 years." DeMaria was supported by four witnesses, all family.

Flaugh was his only witness and despite my critical cross-examination, he was unmoved. His defense was simply that he in fact had borrowed the money, it was a political loan, but it was from Tony Mendela: "I don't recall the vivid details. As far as I was concerned, I borrowed it from Tony Mendela," was the gist of his testimony.

I never could understand why the mayor did not repay the money and avoid the trial. It took the jury 20 minutes to return a verdict against the mayor and again there was voluminous newspaper coverage. It was beginning to be said my cases were providing front-page news coverage grist competing with national news for front-page space on the local paper. I was good copy for the newspaper and I certainly was fully rewarded. These stories of my trials were making my name one to consider for any prospective litigant for miles around my Niles office.

REPRESENTATION FOR AND AGAINST LAW ENFORCEMENT PERSONNEL

In that same period, it was not uncommon of me to sharply and publicly criticize whoever locally exceeded his official responsibility, and this was not limited to public officials. In 1953, Joseph Sieber was a young man, 27 years of age, a Korean War veteran who had served as a Berrien County Deputy Sheriff and he was the first Police Chief of Benton Township, Berrien County, Michigan. He was to become a very popular, highly respected and able law enforcement officer. On September 10, 1953, one James Kemp had been taken without warrant into custody and was being questioned by Chief Sieber in the Berrien County Jail. Kemp was a 21-year old cripple, a victim of muscular paralysis since the age of 6 years, a condition which prevented normal growth. He had a normal head on a shrunken body. He was unable to walk and had to be carried wherever he went. He was forced to sit up in order to accommodate his

deformed condition. The youth was suspected of the theft and possession of a pistol. The authorities suspected a juvenile burglary ring. Sieber
had carried on the interrogation for 45 minutes or more. Not being satisfied with the youth's answer and frustrated and irritated at Kemp's refusal to admit his involvement, he had slapped the boy about the face
several times with the back of his hand in order to force a confession.

Kemp's mother asked me to intercede for him. I promptly demanded that Sieber be reprimanded. Joseph Killian, the County Prosecutor, for whom I must confess I bore no affection, did issue simulta-
neously an assault warrant against Sieber and a warrant against Kemp
for having possession of stolen property under the value of $50, a misde-
meanor charge. Chief Sieber promptly entered a plea of guilty to the
assault charge and was assessed a $25 fine and costs. He issued a public
statement saying that Kemp continued his protestations of innocence,
even after being confronted by the confessions of others implicating him,
and after 45 minutes of lies, he had slapped the youth to get a confession.
He promised in his statement to "continue being a Police Chief of Benton
Township to build up the department for the people who want law enforcement."

The prosecutor in issuing his warrant against young Kemp had,
in a public statement reported widely in the press, branded him as a
"leader of a youthful gang of hoodlums and a 'fagin' with a long record
of involvement in crime, who had lied to Officer Sieber and under such
provocation, the officer in slapping the boy was guilty only of a technical assault."

In my representation of Kemp, a plea of innocence was filed
before the magistrate within 24 hours of Chief Sieber's plea of guilty to
the assault charge. I was furious with the prosecutor.

The police officer was certainly wrong in slapping the crippled
boy during the interrogation but he had promptly pleaded guilty and
paid his dues. Too, despite the welling support of his community, there
were critical voices being raised and the officer was understandably concerned that his job might be in jeopardy. The prosecutor however was

first and last a lawyer who should have been sensitive to the requirement that he not taint or poison the atmosphere of the area where his prosecution of a misdemeanor charge, or indeed any charge, against the crippled boy would take place with a strong prosecutorial prejudgment bias. This was wholly unfair and would deny the youth the opportunity to defend himself before an impartial judge or jury. It angered me the more that the prosecutor had seen fit to irresponsibly make such statement involving a mere misdemeanor warrant which he had authorized. That did not augur well, should a more serious charge be presented against anyone in Berrien County. A prosecutor should try his case in Court and not in the press. The prosecutor having taken his case to the press, I felt compelled to do the same. I released a press statement in which I decried the actions of the authorities who had issued press statements designed to enflame the minds of the public against Kemp and prejudge him before his trial. The full text of my statement was as follows:

"I have every confidence that James Kemp will secure a fair trial in Berrien County on the charge for which he is arrested. That is his right and that is a Berrien tradition. He has pleaded innocent to this charge and he certainly should not be prejudged. I am very concerned about the irresponsible statements of some public officials which would infuse an atmosphere of prejudice and prejudgment in these proceedings. The statement of a police chief guilty reprehensibly of police brutality seeking to justify his conduct must be understood in its proper light. A prosecutor should not, however, prior to presenting evidence, seek to so enflame the public mind by the bandying about of labels like 'fagin' or 'youthful gang leader' and other irresponsible statements so as to infringe the Defendant's right to a fair and judicious determination of his guilt or innocence. It is past time this sort of activity stop."

The charges against Kemp never were brought to trial and were to be dismissed by the prosecutor subsequently. I had branded the charges that Kemp knew about the pistol or made any admission regarding it as false. When the charges were dismissed by the prosecutor I demanded a public apology from the authorities and the prosecutor for the statements made about the youth when he was arrested. My statement release to the press was as follows:

"The action of the authorities in dismissing the warrant against the crippled boy, James Kemp, which was issued midst a flurry of statements branding him a 'fagin' and a 'leader of a gang of hoodlums' and declaring the action necessary to protect the public, would appear at the very least to call for an apology. This should go to a boy who simply asked for the chance to clear himself through trial of the charges against him, but was never given that opportunity."

Prosecutor Killian never commented on my public demand for an apology and he gave none. Kemp, contrary to the prosecutor's statement, when the warrant was issued, never in fact had any record of criminal involvement.

Not willing to leave the matter lie, I brought suit for Kemp against Chief Sieber and his bonding company, filing a complaint in the Berrien County Circuit Court for $5,000 damages for the assault. This case ultimately was to be settled out of court for $1,000. In the process I had struck a blow for responsible law enforcement and I had no doubt that I was mirroring the public sense of outrage against police brutality, when it was exposed, and prosecutorial excess zeal outside the Court room of criminal prosecutions.

WIN SUIT AGAINST GM: Four Chicago women were awarded total of $162,637 Friday by Berrien Circuit Court jury for injuries sustained in 1972 car crash resulting from defective part in auto manufactured by General Motors. Judgment went against GM and two other defendants. Winning damages were (front row from left) Winifred Dorscheid, 84, and Dorothy Loskill, 78. In back (from left) are Florence Mathews, 73, and Dorothy Idell, 71. (Staff photo)

THE ASSOCIATION OF TRIAL LAWYERS OF AMERICA

Editor in Chief
THOMAS F. LAMBERT, JR.
145 Pinckney Street, Suite 728
Boston, Massachusetts 02114
(617) 523-1416

Aug. 14, 1992

George S. Keller, Esq.
Compleat Advocate
Keller Law Building in Centre Court
814 Port St., P.O. Box 7
St. Joseph, MI   49085

Dear George:

   Deepest thanks to you for your thoughtfulness in sending me copy of your volumes of memoirs, View from the Top, a treasure trove of deeply wise insights, combat-tested, into the art and science of advocacy.

   To adopt a figure of Mr. Justice Holmes, the volume gathers together fragments of your golden fleece scattered upon the hedgerows of your life.

   If it would not be too much trouble, could you have your secretary send me a copy of p. 110 of the volume inadvertently omitted from the copy kindly sent to me.

   It must be a source of legitimate pride to have had such a shaping hand in influencing the contours and content of both the public and private law of Michigan and the nation.

Best,
Sincerely,
Tom Lambert

1050 31ST STREET, N.W., WASHINGTON, D.C. 20007   202/965/3500

STATE OF MICHIGAN

MICHIGAN STATE POLICE

EAST LANSING

April 26, 1961

Mr. George S. Keller
Attorney at Law
111 North Fourth St.,
Niles, Michigan

Dear Mr. Keller:

As you no doubt realized, personnel of our Department kept me informed as to the progress of the trial in the case of John Ackerman vs. Lemual Mangold and John Slattery. I have also been informed as to the extremely significant and important contributions you made in the successful defense of Officer Mangold and Trooper Slattery.

I wish to convey my sincere appreciation and profound gratitude to you for having represented Officer Mangold without any financial recompense. In this case, we felt a responsibility to Officer Mangold as he was, at our request, assisting one of our Troopers. Our feeling of indebtedness also recognizes that your activities in this trial resulted in an overlapping situation, where as a matter of fact you were also defending Trooper Slattery.

Lieutenant Donald E. Oates told me that one of the highlights of the defense was your astute cross examination of the witnesses. I understand that you made the closing argument to the jury for both of the defendants. The theme of your closing argument of unbelief and then belief on the part of parties involved and using as a pattern of logical presentation chapters of a book was most effective.

On the next occasion that I am in Niles, I hope to be able to meet you personally. If at any time in the future I may be of service to you, please do not hesitate to call me. Thank you again for your work in our behalf.

Sincerely,

Joseph A. Childs

COMMISSIONER

JAC.doe

Farm Is Scene Of Shooting

Boy Discovers Fired Worker Beneath Bed

By DEWEY HANES
N-P Staff Writer

A 17-year-old Baroda farm youth described by his minister as a "good boy," faces a first degree murder charge today for the shotgun slaying of a man he caught hiding in his mother's bedroom.

The shooting took place about 1 a.m. Sunday in the living room of the Hattie Schmaltz farm home two miles south of Baroda on Miller road.

Held at the Berrien county jail on the murder count is Dennis Lee Schmaltz, whose widowed mother owns the 60-acre farm. The boy's father died four years ago.

Berrien sheriff's detectives said Schmaltz admits firing a 20-guage shotgun blast that hit Theodore Alfred (Shorty) Barton, 58, in the lower abdomen at close range. Barton was dead on arrival at Memorial hospital in St. Joseph.

FORMER EMPLOYE

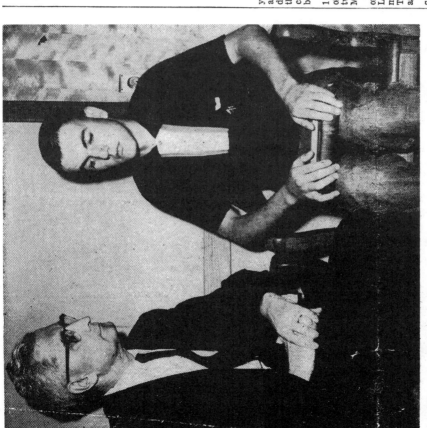

QUIET AND MEDITATIVE, 17-year-old Dennis Lee Schmaltz, (right), clutches Bible as he talks to his minister, Rev. M. J. Michael, of Trinity Lutheran church of Glendora, at Berrien county jail. The teenager is charged with murder for the shotgun slaying of Theodore Barton, 58, early Sunday at the Schmaltz farm home near Baroda. (News-Palladium photo)

FARM HOME south of Baroda where 17-year-old Dennis Schmaltz shot and killed former hired hand he found hiding in his mother's bedroom early Sunday. Sheriff's officers said the victim, 58-year-old Theodore Barton, climbed into house through bedroom window. Story on front page. (News-Palladium photo)

The South Bend Tribune, Tuesday, October 18, 1960.

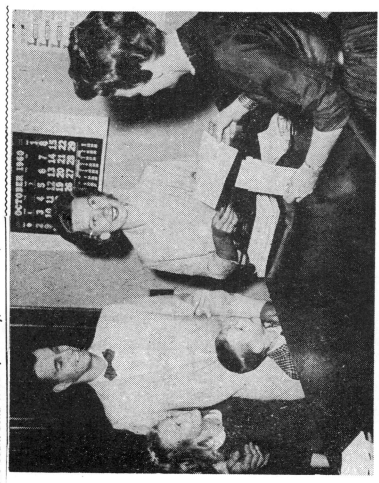

BRIDGMAN HOUSEWIFE WINS LONG COURT BATTLE OVER SPEEDING COUNT—Mrs. Evelyn Konya accepts a receipt for bond money she posted on appealing a justice of the peace court speeding conviction to the Berrien County Circuit Court. The money is being returned by Mrs. Beatrice Tieffenbach, right, deputy county clerk, after a circuit court jury reversed the lower court conviction and acquitted her of the charge. Looking on are Mrs. Konya's husband, Frank, and their two children, Kathleen, 8, and Kevin, 5.

—Photo by Tribune Staff Photographer.

FATHER ACQUITTED—Wednesday was a memorable day for Ross Williams who sits on his father's lap. Ross celebrated his second birthday and his father, Fred W., was found innocent in Circuit court of resisting arrest. Other members of the Benton township family are Jeannie, 6, and Mrs. Williams.

★   ★   ★   ★   ★   ★

Is Found Innocent Of Resisting Arrest

It took less than an hour and one-half of deliberation Wednesday for a Berrien county circuit court jury to find Fred W. Williams, 30, of 1055 Indiana ave., Benton township, innocent of resisting arrest.

Williams' acquittal was announced by the jury foreman at 2:24 p.m., and ended a 2½ day trial on charges brought by Benton Harbor police.

The not guilty verdict by the six-man, six-woman jury followed final arguments Wednesday morning by Prosecutor Ronald Lange and Williams' attorney, George Keller, of Niles.

The charges against Williams arose from a March 1 incident at Pipestone and Britain, in Benton Harbor, when Benton Harbor Patrolman Harry Lenardson stopped Williams' car for failure to have 1964 license plate tabs.

Testimony at the trial as to what followed differed great-ly, and was termed by Lange "a mass and myriad of conflicting testimony."

Atty. Keller, in a dramatic summation, claimed that Williams was subjected to unreasonable and unlawful search and seizure, and was beaten by police. He said Williams did not resist arrest.

Atty. Lange said there was "abundant evidence from every point at the scene that Williams knowingly and unlawfully resisted and assaulted (Officer) Lenardson."

Attorney Acquitted Of Assault

FOUND INNOCENT: Myron Minuskin (center), a Chicago attorney, huddles with his wife, Marsha, and his attorney, George Keller, after being acquitted by Berrien Circuit court jury on charge of assault with a dangerous weapon. (Staff photo)

Chicago Atty. Myron Minuskin, 37, was acquitted by a Berrien Circuit court jury Friday of assault with a dangerous weapon after eight days of trial, one of the longest here in recent memory.

After hearing the verdict, Minuskin wept briefly, kissed his wife of almost 20 years, Marsha, and wept again.

He was charged by Berrien Prosecutor Ronald Taylor with using a .25-caliber pistol to assault an admitted Michigan City prostitute, Sharon Jean Kelley, at the Minuskin summer home at Union Pier on Dec. 11, 1967.

Minuskin testified on the day of the alleged offense he visited a friend in Indiana and a horse stable n e a r Michigan City, drove to the Union Pier home and was robbed of $250 at gunpoint by what he believed to

BENEFITS OF
SOLO PRACTICE

The solo practitioner has considerably more control of his time, much more leeway as to his attitudes, and opportunity to indulge in idiosyncrasies than a lawyer involved in a partnership. I was to practice solo until my son, Jack Keller, graduated from law school and we formed a partnership in 1960. To some extent thereafter, and I must agree very substantially after I had moved into my new office in St. Joseph in 1972, I was not the free spirit I had been prior thereto.

During that solo period, I developed many habits which today would not be permissible in an association with other lawyers. Early in the '40's I became a committed nonsmoker, probably about the time the Surgeon General of the United States had publicly announced the connection between cancer and smoking. I refused to permit anyone in my office or indeed in my home to smoke cigarettes or cigars. I went well beyond the typical nonsmoker posture. I really became belligerent. I refused to represent a client who smoked! Oddly I never lost a client because of my rigid attitude. On an average of 7 to 10 a week, for 25 to 30 years, they took the pledge with me to abstain for a period of six months. About the courtrooms and the courtroom facilities the smokers were putting their cigarettes behind their backs or seeking shelter from me, because I was somewhat of a fanatic and had no hesitancy in pulling cigarettes away from fingers and launching into a monologue of the dangers of nicotine. Sheriffs deputies, judges, prosecutors, attorneys, and clients, I gathered them all in the same net. Attorney Jerry O'Connor, a capable trial lawyer in nearby Cassopolis, who had been a Cass County Prosecutor and with whom I had frequent courtroom contests, was a confirmed chainsmoker. I unrelentingly pursued him every time I saw him over a period of some 20 years. He was gentle in his evasive tactics and entirely a gentleman.

I was belligerently hostile. Poor Jerry at the end was to ask me to give him the pledge. He was ill with cancer and cardiac problems. He was most sincere in taking the abstention pledge for approximately six months. For that period so strong was the strength of the habit on him that wherever he went. he had an unlit cigarette clenched between the first and second fingers of his right hand. After a while, it became a very unpleasant sight. The cigarette turned sickly green and repulsive. To no avail. It was too late and Jerry died in the 1970's. His name, to all who knew him, was a tragically added statistic to the cigarette death toll.

I dealt only with men. I discovered that if a man smoked, his wife typically did not and she would ally herself with me in compelling the husband to be quit of the habit. Men are known procrastinators, putting off many times what they ought to do. Most men, I believe, at one or another time in their lives, make a determination to quit smoking on some future date. I was simply the catalyst who pushed them into making a decision. I believed women to be stronger characters and, if addicted to a habit of this nature, were not as prone to listen to reason or any prodding from another, especially from a man.

A typical incident that I can relate occurred in my Niles office over a weekend. My wife Rachel was in the outer office. A man, his wife and three daughters were consulting me in my private office. He was devastated for he had lost his only son to a drunken automobile driver and he had asked me to assume the wrongful death cause of action. Needless to say, as a personal injury plaintiff's lawyer, I wanted to assume the case.

The man paced the floor in his grief. He knew of my stricture against smoking in the office and at several short intervals he would leave the office and smoke outside. His wife and children were to tell me their grief the result of the loss of a son and brother was compounded by their concern for husband and father. When the man came back into my office I was blunt with him. I would not assume the case of his deceased son unless he pledged with me total abstinence for six months from tobacco. If he was not able to do that he could find other counsel. I took about eight minutes to quickly tell him what I knew about the medical correlation between smoking, lung cancer and cardiac complications, emphysema and a host of other problems. I literally took him through the autopsy of a lung cancer victim and portrayed the grayish lung with its diminished capacity to filter and give oxygen to the blood the result of nicotine ingestion.

The man was livid! He had come to me for the purpose of assuming his son's wrongful death action and not to hear a sermon. He would have no part of it. Though he did not yet realize it, he was on the losing end of the confrontation. I had been talking not only to him, but over his head to his wife and children and they quickly teamed up with me against him. "Do it, Dad, we want you to do it," pled the children. The wife, concerned for her husband, vigorously came to my aid. The pledge was taken and the family joined in the commitment. The wrongful death cause was successfully to be resolved. What I remember most about the case however was the family confrontation in my office.

My wife Rachel, who had been witness to the incident, felt I had been cruel and she was unremitting for a long time in her opposition to my method.

I was to discover, however, that clients who seek out a lawyer, do so because of their trust in his judgment and their willingness to follow his advice. My rationale was if the client did not follow my advice in this critical regard, I had no confidence I would be able to be of service to him. I seldom, if ever, asked women to take the pledge because they are more adamant smokers. Men seem to be more conscious of the danger and easier to convince. I simply was pushing them in the direction of taking a step they had too long deliberated.

When my son and I opened up a new office in St. Joseph in the mid '60's I insisted that no employee, associate or partner be permitted to smoke in our offices. I should have preferred to administer a pledge to one and all with respect to the nicotine habit outside the office, but I was overruled. I soon discovered that other partners were having smoking clients puff their cigarettes outside the office in a little anteroom by the exit door. In my spare time I frequently pulled these poor devils, who I feared would suffocate, into my office and for free gave them my eight minute lecture, returning them to my bemused partners, having one less problem.

Over a period of active practice, I estimate conservatively I gave the pledge to approximately 15,000 or more men. Obviously many may have lapsed back to the habit. I am convinced however that the majority made it. Many years after I had given the pledge to them, a great number of these people have phoned or written me thanking me for literally pushing them so as to take the commitment.

Another idiosyncrasy of mine was to insist on answering my own phone. I wanted any client of mine to be able to reach me easily without running the gauntlet of secretary, delay and call back. It was a simpler era and the multipartner law office cannot so operate. In that era, however, my clients appreciated their being able to promptly contact me first by reaching for the phone.

Another rule of mine would horrify the modern practitioner. I never sent a billing or statement of fees rendered to any client! The proceeding in most of my cases involved contingency fees and clients received their money from me, not the other way around. There were many other consultations and services for which fees were expected to be paid. I had the odd attitude, odd as I reflect on it now, in the context of present practice, that when I finished a consultation for any service, I expected the client to ask me how much he owed. If he did not ask me, he frequently left my office without being told. Fortunately for me I did not have many clients who failed to ask. But it did happen that months after, and in some instances years later, a client would call to say that he had never received a billing and did not know what my fees were and if he had been told he would have paid them. I would consider that an inquiry as to how much, tell him, and I never failed to receive the amount due.

To the young lawyer today, I have no justification for the practice which now would be regarded as quixotic. Today microcomputer statement billing processors are available for monthly mailings. My rationale was that I was attracting sufficient clientele who were satisfied with my services and paid for them. I did not want to be overly concerned with accounts receivable.

Whether or not other attorneys of that day could make sense of those oddities, individually or in combination, they did serve to afford my practice a unique character which together with success in Courtroom dramatics, was to singularly give me a reputation as an attorney who attracted many clients. My clients became attached to me with a warmth that was my best recommendation. Farmers brought gifts of fruit and vegetables in season and one client gave me a leather Hartman attaché case which I was to use for over 20 years. The profession became not only an occupation, it became a hobby which I thoroughly enjoyed. I was to look to courtroom activity as the only satisfying experience of a lawyer. Time spent in the office was secondary and cases were coming which required my activity far removed from my office and indeed from my county.

A cause early in the '50's which drew my support among many others was the case of Evelyn Konya. There really was no fee involved, rather I was drawn to it on the basis of sheer principle. Over a $2 speeding fine, I ultimately was to take the case from a J.P. Magistrate Court to a full 12 member Circuit Court jury, something in our county no attorney had ever done before and certainly none has done since.

Mrs. Evelyn Konya of Bridgman, Michigan, wanted to contest a

$2 speeding charge and I agreed to represent her. I do not believe a fee was even discussed. Evelyn was a Girl Scout den mother and on April 20, 1960, she was driving through Baroda, Michigan, enroute home from a den meeting. In the car were her two children, Kathleen, age 8 years, and Melvin, age 5 years. As she passed various speed limit signs in a 25 mile an hour zone, she explained to her children the meaning of those signs and how they should be obeyed by good citizens. She showed them how her speedometer was reflecting her obedience to the signs. She was giving the youngsters an object lesson in citizen discipline and the necessity to obey laws.

As she was explaining the speed limits, a motorcycle policeman came up from behind and drew alongside the car, commanding her to pull over. The officer told her she had been speeding which she vehemently denied. He took her to the Baroda Justice of the Peace. There he pressed the charge saying that he had clocked her at 55 miles per hour in a 25 mile per hour zone, but was only charging her with 45 miles. When Mrs. Konya protested that she was not speeding and the traffic violation points — which had become routine in Michigan at the time — would unfairly be placed on her record, the Justice of the Peace told her the case would not involve the state point system. He only sent to Lansing reports of drunken and reckless driving!

She was indignant for many reasons. The charge of speeding was false, and worse, the officer and magistrate to her discerning eye were practicing a speed trap operation. The officer was miffed when she said she would not plead guilty. He remarked that he had arrested many speeders (*sic*) and no one had ever questioned the arrest. It was as though he was adding up a score of notches on his gun handle. Both the officer and magistrate pointed out that it was nothing but a $2 speeding ticket which would not be reported the State. Why therefore make the fuss?

I shared her sense of outrage and went with her to the office of the Justice of the Peace in Baroda. The Justice had never had a jury panel and he was surprised when told him I could not possibly trust the decision to him and required a jury. I went through the statutes with him to select a village jury, the first ever empaneled in Baroda before a Justice of the Peace. Finally a jury was sworn, despite the fact most of them seemed to be friends, or at least acquaintances of either the officer or the Justice of the Peace. I had the sneaking suspicion that there were some poker playing buddies of either the constable or the magistrate on that jury. Despite my best efforts, the jury found Mrs. Konya guilty and her $2 fine had now swollen with costs to $31.35.

Neither Mrs. Konya or I was content to let the matter lie at that level. She was eager to appeal and her husband agreed. I appealed the case of the "wrongly accused speeding den mother" to a Berrien County jury. She was required to post bond on appeal just like any convicted misdemeanant. I could have waived jury but we both wanted the exposure of a jury trial and I was ready to make a dramatic presentation.

On the day of the trial, at my suggestion, not only Mrs. Konya's den of girl scouts, but several other dens, with the members all in uniforms were seated in the Courtroom. We had determined that a public trial exposing the manner in which Mrs. Konya had been charged with the false speeding charge, urged to plead guilty, and take a small fine with promise of no points lost, would be a stunning object lesson to the children in civic responsibility and good citizenship. Judge Thomas Robinson, by now a favorite of mine, for I respected his no-nonsense approach, commented that he had never seen a $2 speeding charge tried to a jury, but in no way was the time and facilities of the Court system being improperly employed.

The jury of 10 women and 2 men was empaneled. It was a far distant proceeding from the 6 man J.P. jury hearing before the magistrate. The magistrate and the police officer were now on trial. The special prosecutor for Baroda had a weak case and he knew it. The constable was his only witness and he was no comfort to the prosecutor. As I reflect now, it was a very uneven contest. Mrs. Konya's two beautiful children, a little girl in her Girl Scout uniform went on stand with the brother and both told how their mother, by her example, was training them to obey traffic signs, obey the laws and be good citizens when the motorcycle cop rode alongside and stopped their car. Evelyn Konya related how both the officer and the magistrate had told her there would be no reporting to the State of her speeding charge and that it was no big thing with only a $2 fine. She expressed her resentment as a citizen.

The jury was out for 20 minutes and returned a verdict of not guilty to the satisfaction of everyone in the Courtroom. The magistrate had not taken the stand though he was later to comment to the press, which found the entire proceedings a fascinating change of pace, that he still believed Mrs. Konya was speeding when given the ticket and she was only concerned about her standing in the community and how many points would appear on her record. He was also to comment he would in the future send notices of all traffic violations to the Secretary of State's office! I was always convinced that the motorcycle constable and the Justice of the Peace magistrate had a burgeoning and profitable speed trap operation in the Baroda area, which I had some influence in cracking.

The press gave lead story and news photo coverage of the Konya family, including the two children looking proudly at their mother receiving back from the Berrien County Clerk the refund of her appeal bond under the caption: BRIDGEMAN HOUSEWIFE WINS LONG COURT BATTLE OVER SPEEDING COUNT. She and her husband were thrilled and satisfied with the result. I had, with little or no payment of any fees, secured full satisfaction for a client who had been victimized by a crooked situation. The newspaper coverage was worth at least the equivalent of $25,000 fee in referrals. It was a far better technique of attracting clients than hanging out and waiting in my law office.

CASES INVOLVING POLICE MATTERS

It was not infrequent that I was called upon to represent citizens who complained of "police brutality." One such incident involved Ross Williams, a house mover who during World War II had been in the Marine Corps and as an extracurricular activity, and been recognized the Marine boxing champion of the Southwest Pacific Theater. He was a husky, well-built and athletic fellow and one with whom no one would have been wise to physically tangle.

One Sunday, March 1, 1964, he was enroute to church with his wife and two children. He had carelessly failed to attach the required 1964 license plates to his automobile, though he had them in the car. He was stopped by Benton Harbor Police who demanded his driver's license and registration. They ordered him out of the car. He had $2,400 in an envelope in his pants pocket which he had collected for a house moving contract and he was concerned that it not be confiscated by the police, whom he did not trust. They stood him against his car and proceeded to frisk and search him. Williams kept his hands tightly gripped to his sides, preventing the police from searching his pockets. He resented the police tactic and if he had chosen, could have flattened the two officers easily. In the process, the police beat and abused him and one of the officers radioed for assistance. A crowd assembled around the officers as they proceeded to attempt to search Williams and were abusing him. Some in the crowd protested the treatment by the police. His wife who was also in the crowd added her pleas to the police to stop beating her husband. At one point she was able to push forward to a position near her husband and he reached in his pocket, extracted the money envelope and give it to her. Then he raised his hands, quit his "resistance." Handcuffed, he was led away. The police claimed that Williams had resisted arrest and assaulted them! The prosecutor authorized criminal complaint and there followed a bizarre sequence in which the prosecution carried the charge all the way to the Circuit Court level.

The pride of our system of law is that a citizen charged with a crime has the constitution-given right to defend himself against excesses of governmental agents in open court. The legal profession's noblest purpose is to intercede and provide counsel for the accused, oppose arbitrary and excessive actions of any government agency, including any law enforcement personnel. Thereby a citizen's privileges and rights to live free in a society are protected. America is not just a utopian fantasy. It is real and the courts are there to test, to criticize, to exorcise any intrusion by even the highest government agency of those precious rights of citizenship. Ross Williams' case was that kind of a case to defend. He had some brothers who had gotten in trouble with the police who may have been confused by the name, but he had an impeccable record as a sober, hard-working, and law abiding person. The police were wrong in treating him the way they did over a technical license plate charge. Their arrest of him on drummed up charges of resisting arrest patently covered up their own misguided zeal and required a vigorous defense.

At the Circuit Court jury trial the officers said Williams was excited when he came out of his car and then got back in and refused to give his identification. The police officer said he did radio for assistance and when the Defendant got out of his car, proceeded to search him and he resisted. A large crowd assembled and the spectacle of a scuffle with excited officers did ensue. The key question was whether Williams was arrested before or after the attempted search. Williams and others testified there was no arrest, simply the call and response for identification, and the attempted search outside the car.

The prosecutor, plainly ill-at-ease, termed the testimony a "mass and myriad of conflicting testimony." He argued that Williams knowingly and unlawfully resisted and assaulted the police officers.

I argued the two officers had conducted an illegal search of Williams' person during which the latter had simply hung on to his large sum of money to keep it from being confiscated by men in uniform who were beating and abusing him. He did not resist arrest. He did resist an unreasonable search of his person to protect his own property. I commented to the jury the "golden diamond-studded right to be let alone" enjoyed by American citizens, and said police had violated Federal and Michigan Constitutional Safeguards against unreasonable search and seizure. We do not live in a police state and no man, because he wears a uniform, has any special right to abuse a citizen. This was the message articulated to the jury panel. These police were historical "bully boys" and were using Williams for a punching bag, I argued. The jury agreed by acquitting Williams in less than one hour. I did not leave it there; I brought suit for damages in the amount of $10,000 against the City of Benton Harbor, and the case was settled out of court.

I thoroughly believed in the required condemnation of those police tactics. I was not however to limit myself to criticism of police officers, because it was well known my services were *pro bono* offered to police or fire personnel who deservedly required them, and I had on many occasions ranged my services on their side.

Edward Lyons, a black officer of the New Buffalo Police Department, charged with an assault and battery, involving a truant 15-year old girl who had run away from home, was charged with having struck her with a rubber strap. Officers testified she was apprehended May 17, 1972. She punched the Chief of Police in the mouth and swore and struggled with the other officers, including Lyons, who came to their help. She admitted she had told the chief if she had a switchblade she would have killed Lyons and she peppered all of the officers with obscenities, calling Lyons a "nigger," a "pig," and a "queer." She had to be subdued, handcuffed and driven to the police post. There was testimony that Lyons, who was also a paramedic, went to the girl thinking she needed medical attention for a cut lip. He removed the handcuffs thinking that might calm her. She resumed hurling ethnic slurs at him, kicked at him in the groin and scratched and bit his arm, drawing blood. Lyons, being highly upset, shook her and reached for a strap on the wall to use against the lower part of her leg which caused her to scream to let up. He was to testify negatively in response to my question: "Did you ever patch her up?" To the question by the prosecutor: "Did you feel you were defending yourself or were you punishing her?" He answered with evident candor:

"Defending myself? I would not say totally either one. My attitude at the time was, I didn't have to take this and I simply swatted her upside her butt and let them get her out of here."

The girl's testimony she was struck on the arms, leg and breast were challenged by medical testimony. Many witnesses testified to Lyons as an officer and paramedic of high repute. He was credited with saving five lives the preceding two years. He was said many times to have volunteered his time and effort for worthy city causes and he was so well- and favorably known by the Berrien County District Court Judges they disqualified themselves. A Van Buren jurist was to preside and acquit him in a nonjury trial. The judge commented that Lyons admitted he had hit the girl two maybe three times to protect himself from her after she had kicked at his groin, bit his leg, and scratched his arm, drawing blood and insulting his race. "Lyons", said the judge, "underwent unbelievable abuse and used allowable force to protect himself."

This was a cause any attorney could assume *pro bono* for the good of society. The officer deserved a vigorous defense against a prosecution which should never have been authorized. After hearing the verdict, Lyons, in tears, said he was discouraged with police work and after eight years on the force, was looking for other employment. Police have to know citizens are on their side and ready to support responsible, vigorous enforcement of the laws. Police are citizens first and have rights of their own which are deserving of every protection.

There were many times I was asked to intercede for the police but the most interesting one was the case of John Ackerman, a Three Oaks apple farmer, who sued Three Oaks patrolman Lemuel Mangold and State Trooper John Slattery for damages, which he claimed resulted from an incident on his premises October 9, 1958. Ackerman claimed that three youths were stealing cider from barrels in his front yard and he had taken out his double-barreled rifle and was holding them prisoner at gunpoint on his property that night. A mother of one of the youths had called the Three Oaks Police and the latter had asked the State Police to assist. The farmer had refused to put down the gun when approached by the officers who identified themselves. In the struggle, he was hit over the head with the barrel of the gun, subdued, handcuffed and taken into custody.

When released on bail the farmer had approached Prosecutor Joseph Killian who referred the matter to Kalamazoo Attorney John Doyle who brought suit for damages against the two officers in Circuit Court. Mangold asked me to defend him and I agreed *pro bono* to do so. The State of Michigan was in dire financial straits and had no trial personnel to represent the state trooper. An Assistant Attorney General was sent down from Lansing but he had had no trial experience and in effect I was called on *pro bono* to represent both officers.

Ackerman gave his version of what happened on the stand and he said he had clear recall of events leading up to the struggle for the gun but he was not fully conscious after he had been hit on the head. He was to testify that the gun anyway did not work and had not been fired in 20 years. He has brought it out to have "a little fun" and play a joke on the three youths who he claimed were stealing his cider at the front yard by the road. While the boys were drawing cider from the barrels he said he removed the ignition key from their car so that they could not leave.

When they tried to pay for the cider he refused to accept payment. He was to insist that in the fight with the officers, the latter assaulted him and the arrest on his own property was unwarranted. He claimed he was seriously injured and unable to work his farm as a result of his injuries. He asked $25,000 damages, a large sum at the time of the trial in 1961, all based on an unwarranted invasive intrusion on his property and assault.

State Trooper Slattery, the main witness for the defense, was on the stand for three hours. He testified that Ackerman refused to put down the gun during the struggle and threatened to 'bash in' the officer's head. The Trooper managed to disengage the barrels from the stock of the gun while Mangold held the farmer's arms and they wrestled the gun barrels away from him. After releasing his hold on the barrels, Ackerman had run towards the farm house and shouted he was going to get a real shotgun and "really do the job." The irate farmer was no longer playing a joke! Slattery knew he somehow had to stop him . He ran after him with barrels in his grip and hit the farmer over the head as he saw the farmer's hand reach out for the door. He was to testify that he had taken the barrels and the stock of the shotgun away from the farmer because he feared for the safety of those with him as well as for his own life. He believed Ackerman was reaching for another gun. A farm employee was to testify that the officers had identified themselves as such to Ackerman before the struggle for the gun.

I made the argument to the jury for both officers and I was to tell the panel in effect that the case of the embattled farmer against the officers trying to maintain order and save lives was built of dust and should end in dust. The jury deliberated less than one hour to reach a no cause in favor of the officers and the *News Palladium,* picking up my summation, headlined the story, "FARMERS SUIT AGAINST OFFICERS GETS HEAVE HO."

Pro bono representation of police did not get fees for me, but recognition of my services, fee-free to law enforcement agencies throughout the State, was a very satisfactory substitute. The State Police Commissioner wrote me a letter of congratulations.

I was to be appointed one of three Michigan citizens of a panel to serve for several years and to nominate awards for the "best trooper in the state." The good will of law enforcement personnel is a precious assist to any trial lawyer. It must never be abused and can only be earned by integrity and a healthy concern for officers who risk their lives in the line of duty.

GENERAL CRIMINAL CASES

In the big cities of the era, criminal defense was considered unfavorably by the general practitioner. It was a facet of the practice, considered somehow to be less than first rate and not befitting the regular trial advocate. Unless it was a well-heeled prominent person who was accused and willing to part with a sizable fee, few lawyers were available to defend criminal cases.

I always believed that the defense of citizens charged with a crime and who are deserving of the defense, is the most stimulating and professionally rewarding challenge to the trial lawyer. Here is an opportunity in the Courtroom forum, before judge and jury, to compel the prosecutor to produce convincing proof, satisfying a jury of 12, comprising a cross-section of the community of the basic merit of his accusation of crime. Just because a complaint and warrant is framed in the language of "The People of the State of Michigan vs. John Doe", does not render the accusation sacrosanct and valid. The defense trial lawyer may be the only force in the community to intercept the arrows aimed at his client. The community may, the result of public statements, prosecution leaks, releases and media reporting, be inclined to shortly and uncritically accept the guilt of the accused by assumption, or simply "benign neglect" and disinterest. The defense lawyer has a duty to protect his client, by all means to him properly available, until the prosecution has proven, not just that the defendant is suspect, but that he is guilty of the charged offense beyond reasonable doubt. That posture is basically the separating line between a free democracy and a police state. I have defended to jury trial many scores of criminal cases. I can only herein cite a few.

Over in Cass County, Michigan, a black woman, Robin Gibbs, had been charged with the murder of her husband in July of 1971. The woman had stabbed her husband Jerry with a paring knife under the left armpit. She had taped up the wound with adhesive tape, seeking to succor him and had lifted him into bed. When she awoke the next morning, her husband had expired and she had beside her a corpse. She called the undertaker and the latter, on straightening out the body for burial, discovered the taping under the arm. The sheriff was called.

Only the dramatic proofs in Court would satisfy a jury of the woman's innocence. Her husband was an alcoholic and the wife had many years endured his drunken tirades. She was seated on a stool peeling potatoes for the evening meal and she had told her husband, because he was drunk, he could not drive the family automobile. She would not release the keys to him. One cannot argue with a drunk and can only cajole him somehow. This drunk became infuriated.

He had a right to drive the car and his wife could not deny him that right. He picked up a chair and upended it over his head as he approached her, cursing the while, as he threatened to bring it down on her unless she gave him the keys. The poor woman persisted in her refusal and as the chair sharply lowered, she struck out with her right hand which held the paring knife, to ward off the blow. The man was accidentally stabbed underneath the left armpit. The pathologist testified most of his blood exsanguinated internally in the abdomen and he expired some time in the middle of the night. The jury found the wife innocent of murder or any other crime. A little woman, a case of small moment to the community, but it was resolved in the tradition of American justice.

THE MINUSKIN CASE

A criminal case of startlingly greater proportion and one which was to consume a much longer trial than any I had handled, came to me in early 1970.

Myron Minuskin was a former assistant corporation counsel of the City of Chicago and assigned to the trial of drug cases. A successful young trial lawyer, 37 years of age, married with five children, he was one of the favorites of Mayor Daley and his future deemed assured in 1969. He had a fine home in Chicago and a summer vacation home on Lake Michigan in Union Pier.

During his work with the City of Chicago he had worked closely with the commander and police of the First Precinct in Chicago in the prosecution of drug cases. He was familiar with their many complaints that the Miranda and other Supreme Court rulings handicapped the police in interrogations of suspected felons and their early securing of implicating statements. Under the Miranda rule, officers could not interrogate without first instructing the accused of his right to counsel and to remain silent. Police were complaining that the Miranda rule was 'handcuffing' them.

In December, 1969, Minuskin was to find himself in deep trouble faced with criminal prosecution for assault with a dangerous weapon brought on by newly elected prosecutor Ron Taylor who was determined to prove a major county crime. Minuskin was brought to my office by an attorney in New Buffalo, a close friend of his who vouchsafed his integrity and recommended me as the only trial attorney in the county who could handle the case vigorously. I did not deserve the reference. It was to prove to be an exhausting experience.

Minuskin gave me his version of the events which culminated in his arrest. He had received a fee of $750 in City Court upon completion of a client's matter. He was free that afternoon and the rest of the day. There was a sick Court Reporter friend of his in Indiana he could visit and a debt of $300 he should pay to a farmer near Michigan City, Indiana, for the stabling and feeding of his daughter's pony. Then there was the matter of getting a trick Christmas present for his favorite Commander of the First Precinct. He pondered and it occurred to him that the police complaint about the Miranda Rule could be symbolically addressed by the gimmick gift of a pair of handcuffs. He went to a gun shop patronized by the police, identified himself, and purchased a new pair of handcuffs. His present was going to be a symbolic play on the Miranda Rule. At other Christmases, Minuskin had bought the Commander a General McArthur hat or some other trick outfit. This one was going to be right on target for the Department's bitching about Miranda. He flung the handcuffs on top of the material along with the balance of his fees in his attaché case and he was on his way via I-94 eastbound. He stopped and visited his sick friend in Indiana and then drive to Michigan City to pay his daughter's pony bill. He found no one there home. By the time he got back to Interstate 94, he realized it was 3:30pm Chicago time and he was concerned about the inevitable Dan Ryan expressway, late afternoon bumper-to-bumper press of traffic.

His Union Pier vacation home, closed for the season was only a short 20 miles further east on I-94 and he determined to drive there and check his property. He was driving a late model white Cadillac automobile and he was certain the groundskeeper would spot and recognize his automobile. He drove on and at approximately 5:30 to 6 o'clock he arrived but did not see the grounds guard. Entering his home he went to the bedroom, put on the heat, took out $50 and laid it on the dresser beside his clothes and attaché case. He was tired, nay, he was bushed. He thought he would undress to his shorts, lay resting on the bed for a short nap, call his wife and then return to his Chicago home. He dozed off momentarily to be awakened by a knock at the door.

Thinking it was the groundskeeper who must have recognized his car, he went to the door and opened it. A negro dressed in dark blue jeans stood there. He confronted him with a pearl handled revolver and forced him back into the bedroom. The intruder demanded his money. He insisted that Minuskin open his attaché case and the latter said there was nothing in it but legal papers. The negro demanded more money.

Minuskin was concerned about opening the attaché case. He told me he was revolted because the intruder had confronted him in his own bedroom. He had always counseled and advised his clients that if they were ever confronted by a gun-wielding assailant, to never quarrel, contest or fight, but to quickly give whatever the gunman demanded. He did not follow his own advice. A plan to thwart the thief formulated in his mind. He would open the attaché case, get out the handcuffs, disarm his assailant and handcuff him! The plan had to be carefully executed. He had in one quick maneuver to open the case, clutch the handcuffs, snap them about the man's wrists and knock the gun away from his grasp.

Minuskin went to the attaché case and brought it to a position close to the man. He opened it, letting it and the contents fall as he grasped the handcuffs with his right arm and with the other knocking the gun out of the right hand of the negro. Then he brought his right hand down hard to snap the open handcuff on the intruder's left arm. One cuff snapped shut. The intruder was able to recover his pistol and began pistol-whipping Minuskin viciously about the head, causing blood to flow in great quantity from many head wounds, all the while cursing, "You M__F__, I should kill you." Minuskin, beaten and bleeding, slumped to the floor. The negro ceased the beating and went over to the dresser, took the $50 exposed on the counter and fled.

Minuskin was dazed. He was bleeding profusely. His first thought was to wash off the blood. He lay in the bathing tub, head under the faucet and let the water run off of him for about 20 minutes. Blood stains were to remain clearly visible in the tub. Somewhat relieved, he called the New Buffalo State Police Post, reported that he had been robbed by a negro male intruder, and he gave as an additional item of identification the circumstance that if they found the assailant, he probably would have a handcuff fastened to his left wrist. The officer at the desk must have raised his eyebrows.

The police call completed, Minuskin called his wife, told her briefly that there had been some trouble at the Union Pier home, he had been robbed and he had to wait the completion of the police investigation.

When the police arrived he repeated the above facts and said that if they found the intruder he would be glad to sign a complaint. He was told it might be midnight before the paperwork was completed. Minuskin remained in his home waiting.

About 11 P.M., the police returned. A critical change of alleged circumstances had occurred. They had indeed run across a negro dressed in blue denim dungarees of the general height and hue described by Minuskin. Significantly a pair of handcuffs was dangling from the left wrist of the person, but, the negro was a female! Worst still, there was a warrant for Minuskin's arrest for assault of the negress with a dangerous weapon!

She had told the police a far different version. She was a prostitute plying her trade in Michigan City, Indiana, and as she walked along the street at approximately 5 P.M. a white Cadillac had pulled alongside and she was beckoned over. The white driver had offered her $50 if she would come with him. She accepted the invitation of the $50 and got into the car, placing on the front dash a magazine which she carried with her. She told the police she was driven to a home in the Union Pier area and entered it with the man. He had taken her to the bedroom and asked her to put her hands behind her back so he could handcuff her. She had resisted as it did not seem to comport with her idea of 'fun and games.' She fought and prevented the man from getting both wrists handcuffed but her left hand was indeed cuffed. In the struggle she did fling the dangling cuff about the head of the man bloodying him until he desisted and then she fled. She tried to call for help at several of the neighbors, but only one let her in, and she called her father, a Michigan City Police officer, and told him her plight. She asked him to come and get her. She was on the highway, handcuff dangling, waiting for him, when she was taken into custody by the State Troopers. Shortly thereafter it was reported the father drove up with four other men in his car looking for his daughter.

The case was a very difficult one to defend. I wanted to believe my client. A lawyer cannot represent a client adequately unless he has faith in him and can sincerely articulate that faith to a jury. Juries are quick to sense a phony defense and no jury of mine had ever doubted the sincerity of my presentation of proofs or summation from the evidence. The prosecutor, young Ronald Taylor, recently elected and on to his first big trial, was an aggressive, capable and thoroughly convincing lawyer. He was later to become District Judge, and then Circuit Judge. His predecessor, John Hammond, was convinced of Minuskin's guilt and claimed that at the end of his term when he was first called, in December 1968, he drove to the place where the white Cadillac was parked, and he observed the magazine described by the prostitute on the dashboard. At trial, Hammond was to so testify, though the magazine was never produced, and it was always his opinion that this testimony should have clinched Minuskin's conviction.

I knew I had to figuratively crawl into Minuskin's skin, relive and retrace every one of the events that had occurred, the travel he undertook, the stops along the highway he made, the observations he made of the condition of congested traffic on the Dan Ryan highway at 3:30 p.m., all to feel, test, critique, and articulate his movements that 11th day of December, 1967. It was an exhaustive preparation. I made the trip from Chicago to Union Pier in a similar manner, a half dozen or more times, stopping, verifying the gun shop in Chicago where he had purchased the handcuffs, the discussion he had had with the Court Reporter, stopping at the pony farm in Michigan City, and then driving on to the vacation home in Union Pier. I timed myself from the City Court Building in Chicago enroute all of these stops from the gun shop to the home in Union Pier. I sat down with the police commander of Precinct Number One in Chicago and satisfied myself that a Christmas gimmick handcuff gift was the kind of stunt gift that Minuskin would be expected to pull off on the captain. I talked to everyone I could, including caretakers, several of the neighbors who had refused the negress' entrance to their homes. There was defense material to present.

The prosecution was thorough. Ronald Taylor demonstrated an

appetite for a tough presentation of proofs. The prostitute, a Miss Kelly, dressed in woman's clothing and looking very like a woman, was the key witness for the prosecution. She spoke in a low voice but she was precise in her details. She admitted her profession and said she was walking along a street in Michigan City with a friend about 5 p.m. She had purchased a magazine and was carrying it under her arm when a new white Cadillac drove up and stopped opposite the two women. Kelly said her friend walked on and the white man at the wheel beckoned her to the car and asked her if she would like to earn $50. She identified Minuskin as that man. She continued with the same version she had initially given the police. She agreed on cross-examination she was dressed in a man's dark clothing and had a dark cloth wrapped around her close cropped hair. She agreed she could have looked like a man and indeed been mistaken for one. She said she was willing to engage in normal intercourse but was not into anything "kinky" and the handcuffs turned her off. She fought Minuskin though he got one handcuff on her left wrist. She said she fled the house and went to several neighboring houses to plead for help. One resident let her in and she told how she had phoned her father at that house for help and then walked out to the highway, waiting until help could be dispatched. The police had found her on the highway, handcuff dangling, dressed in a man's blue denims, all fitting the description Minuskin had given them.

Former prosecutor Hammond's testimony was to fit part of the prosecution puzzle. The neighbor at whose home the prostitute made her phone call testified, supporting Miss Kelly in that regard. The father, a police officer of Michigan City, testified to having received the call and having responded by driving to the scene, vainly looking for his daughter. By the time the prosecution had finished his proofs, Minuskin's defense was in peril.

The defense proofs ran into a number of snags. I could not subpoena the Chicago Precinct Number One commander to come to St. Joseph to testify live, for he was not subject to subpoena across a state border. However, he had faithfully promised me he would voluntarily come to the trial and testify on Minuskin's behalf. To my distress and dismay, two days before trial, he wired me he could not come as planned. I called him on the phone and he was to tell me that he had been ordered to stay away from and out of the proceedings. He did not dare disobey. To come to the trial would risk exile from his post, as he put it. I scheduled a deposition to be taken in a Chicago hotel room, something the Circuit Judge had never authorized in a criminal action in Berrien County, and we were to adjourn the jury action until this could be completed. To my surprise a Chicago Tribune reporter showed up at the time of the deposition and insisted on covering it under the guise of "power of the press," all despite my vigorous protest and attempt to evict him from the room. It seemed strange to me that the Chicago Tribune should be interested in a Berrien County Circuit Court trial of Minuskin.

The commander, obviously ill-at-ease with city corporation counsel at his elbow constantly advising his answers, and in many instances urging and securing his non-answer, was grudgingly to admit the handcuff symbolism attached to the Miranda warning requirement, which was resented by the police. The handcuffs were a dangerous-to-defense-chip of the prosecution, and it was critical that they be explained. I had to put them into a plausible frame for the jury to accept. The commander's deposed testimony, though limited extremely, did provide critical support to Minuskin's explanation of his possession of those handcuffs.

During the trial there were a number of mysterious, out-of-town spectators at the back of the Courtroom and Minuskin was to tell me repeatedly that they were planted there by his enemies at Chicago City Hall who were getting daily reports on the trial proceedings which were now going onto the second week, all in the course of planning his eclipse at City Hall. I was beginning to wonder if this was not all part of a huge plot to get at Minuskin.

Minuskin testified that on December 11, 1967, after purchasing the handcuffs as an intended 'gimmick' Christmas present for his Chicago police friend, he had visited the ill court reporter friend in Indiana, had gone on to the horse stable near Michigan City, then drove to his

Union Pier property, and was robbed of $50 at gunpoint by what he believed was a negro male dressed in dark clothing. He had managed to lock a handcuff on one hand of the robber before the latter pistol-whipped him to submission. He denied on cross-examination that there were any passengers in his car or any magazine on the front dashboard of the car and he passionately denied any involvement whatsoever with the prostitute.

The argument given to the jury was intense, both by the prosecutor and myself. The prosecutor had scoffed at the suggestion that the handcuffs could have been used by Minuskin as he claimed. Handcuffs however had been submitted into evidence in the case and I proceeded in argument to demonstrate how they could be flung and snapped on the wrist of another person from a distance. Using an upended chair, I several times snapped the open cuffs at a leg until I caught and snapped on one of the cuffs. I hoped the jury would be convinced, as I was, that this was the manner, as he had testified, that Minuskin had cuffed the intruder's one wrist when he was confronted by this "black male" robbing him at gunpoint in his bedroom on December 11.

I made some mention of how difficult it had been to get the Chicago Police Commander to Court to testify as I would have preferred, but I made sure the jury understood the reason for Minuskin's possession of the handcuffs. They were no piece of perverted sex equipment. They were in fact a gimmick Christmas present the Defendant, a close friend of the officer, was planning to give him that Christmas. Minuskin was the kind of a person possessed of wry humor and wit who would have thought of such a gimmick to amuse and entertain his friends. This whole thing was a ghastly turn of events and the whole had been plotted somehow to bring about the disgrace and collapse of Minuskin's career.

It was not an easy defense to articulate to the jury. Because of my thorough preparation for trial and my frequent consultations with everyone whom I could contact having any connection with Minuskin, I was convinced of his innocence. There was no denying that the prosecution had produced strong evidence placing that innocence in question. I argued if the presumption of Minuskin's innocence was to be stripped from him, the proofs must rise to the level of establishing beyond all possible doubt his guilt. It was no easy task for the jury.

The panel, comprised of seven men and three women, remained out on deliberation almost four hours before they returned with a verdict of acquittal of the charge of assault with a dangerous weapon. Minuskin and his wife, Marcia, wept and embraced. The young prosecutor was bitterly disappointed.

I have always believed that jury duty is one of the most important and satisfying areas of service for citizens. The following Christmas I was to receive a heartwarming confirmation from the "Minuskin jury" which stated as follows:

December 22, 1969

Dear Mr. Keller:

Members of the "Minuskin jury" met together in St. Joseph in November. We all wished you had been there to talk with us.

Not only were we privileged to be "jury Members" this year (April-May), but we felt the Minuskin case was a rare one and the experience of a lifetime for us. We received the added bonus of having formed some fine and sincere friendships.

I know I speak for the entire Jury when I express our admiration for you and wish you a wonderful New Year.

Jeanne Peterson
Member of the Jury

THE BARTON CASE

I had occasion to defend a youth, Ronald Meritt, age 18, charged with an armed robbery of a Benton Township tavern in the late '60's. Merrit was a freshman enrolled at Eastern Michigan University and was identified by the victim from a 1968 Benton Harbor High School yearbook as one of the two principals involved in the robbery. On the basis of that identification, the police had arrested the young man outside of his dormitory at Eastern Michigan University in Ypsilanti. The lad had an impeccable background. He stoutly defended his innocence. We had alibi witnesses to establish his very proper activities of December 1, 1969, the date of the robbery.

I had always suspected that identification of the individual seated as the Defendant beside his counsel at time of trial by the victim of a crime testifying in the case, was too easily made. The Defendant placed next to his attorney was to well marked a target. If the Complainant and prosecution witness on the stand, called to identify and finger the Defendant, has any misgivings, he surely will be apt to resolve those by pointing out the person sitting beside defense counsel.

I determined to test my concern. I had the father of the Defendant, a man 44 years of age who had the same crew cut as the boy, sit beside me at the counsel table. The father was 2 inches shorter, 10 pounds lighter, and 16 years older than the son. I instructed young Ronald Meritt to seat himself among the spectators behind the bar.

When the prosecution witness identified the father beside me as the robber, I was satisfied my concern indeed was a proper one. I rose to my feet and asked that the Defendant, the real Ronald Meritt, rise, which he did from the rear of the room. The prosecutor, nonplused, at once dismissed the charge. He was later to make press comment philosophically of the mistaken identities. "This is not unusual," he said.

The Court was not to be gentle with me. I was warned never again to try that particular maneuver in his court. I never did.

In 1962 a murder case was to be aired with running stories in the press keeping the public stirred full tilt. A 17 year-old Baroda farm boy had shot and killed a farm laborer named Barton, age 58 years he had found in his mother's bedroom. The shooting had taken place at 1 a.m. Sunday, July 15, 1962, in the bedroom of the boy's widowed mother. The boy admitted firing the 20 gauge shotgun that hit the man in the lower abdomen at close range. He was dead on arrival at the hospital. I was retained to defend the youth.

It was to develop at the trial that Barton had been discharged by the mother's sons who helped operate the farm. There was evidence of bad feeling between him and the sons, especially Dennis. It was testified at the trial that Dennis and an older brother had accosted the man at a cabin he had rented after being fired and, brandishing clubs, had warned Barton to stay away from the mother. There was testimony at the trial to be presented by the prosecution that Dennis was aware Barton was a frequent visitor at the home to see his mother. The prosecutor argued that Dennis was the aggressor and he sought to link the mother socially with Barton. She testified she had met Barton accidentally several times after he was fired, at a Bridgman bar, and had gone to his cabin to "admonish him for saying bad things about her." She denied having any social contact with the man after his discharge and testified that she awoke the night of the shooting to find him standing beside her bed, having come through a window. She said she started screaming and her son responded. The man had hidden under the bed and Dennis came into the room with a gun, jumped on the bed and fired a warning shot into the wall. She testified both she and Dennis ran out into the living room and that Barton came out of the bedroom carrying a rolled up blanket in his hands, waving it from side to side, and that Dennis shot him in the leg. The pathologist testified the blast struck Barton in the left thigh severing an artery, causing him to bleed to death.

I argued, seeking acquittal, that Dennis had shot Barton in self-defense. The prosecutor urged the jury to find Dennis guilty of First Degree Murder.

The 14 members of the jury (2 alternates) were taken to view the scene of the homicide to familiarize themselves with the premises. The trial ended with a hung jury, the panel having been out 12 hours for deliberation from 11:40 a.m. until approximately 11:40 p.m. The members unanimously reported they could not agree on a verdict. Circuit Court Judge, Phillip Hadsell, discharged them after admonishing them not to discuss the case with the public, press or anyone else, and specifically not to relate how many were in favor of acquittal or conviction. There was no hint as to whether the majority leaned toward acquittal or conviction. Several of the women jurors appeared to have been crying. A host of friends, relations and well-wishers of young Dennis crowded around him to encourage him. He was free on a $5,000 appearance bond but he was to face a second trial the following term.

A second Berrien County jury was in fact empaneled the end of January 1963 and the ordeal was to be completed.

I was to argue with a passion I felt, the claim of self-defense justifying the homicide. Barton was an intruder in the Schmaltz home and Dennis reasonably believed Barton had come with the intention of harming both his mother and him. The son had fired a warning shot in the wall and had retreated as far as he could into the home upon Barton's menacing advance. The events leading to the shooting had unfolded like the chapters of a book with the "chapter of terror" coming swiftly and terrifyingly upon the boy. Even after Barton had advanced from the bedroom to the living room in pursuit of Dennis, the boy had ordered him to stop and he had fired into the man's leg, not a vital area, in an attempt to halt him, rather than kill him. Why had he used a gun? I pointed out that Dennis had testified that he and Barton had matched strength wrestling while the latter worked on the Barton farm and Dennis had always been bested. Dennis knew Barton was the stronger and that he carried a knife. He had good reason to fear for his life. The gun was the equalizer. the prosecutor was to argue that Dennis was the aggressor. Regardless of his good reputation and character all established by testimony, he was guilty of homicide. The court charged the jury to consider only Second Degree Murder, Manslaughter, or acquittal.

The second jury of seven women and five men took only one hour and 15 minutes. They brought back a verdict of not guilty. All of Dennis' friends were elated. The lad, who had been noncommittal and had shown no emotional facial expression throughout the two proceedings, broke out in a broad smile which must have capped many months of tension.

THE TENNESSEE POTATO CASE

I was called to defend criminal cases outside the State of Michigan a number of times. I will only relate two cases.

In the 1950's, I defended in Coffee County, Tennessee, a truckdriver who, deadheading back north from Florida, had stopped in Manchester to load up his refrigerator truck with U.S. Number One potatoes. He had stopped to check his load in South Bend, Indiana, and found the potatoes decayed and rotten. He dump-sold the load at a commercial grade price at substantial loss and going through Niles, Michigan, stopped to get my advice. I told him to stop payment on the check and wire the potato grower that he would settle on the basis of his sales less transportation costs.

I should not have so blithely advised him, for in Tennessee a check given in such circumstances is regarded equivalent of cash. Ultimately a Tennessee Deputy Sheriff, armed with Writ of Extradition given by Michigan Governor Kim Sigler in response to a Tennessee request for extradition mandated the truckdriver's return to the Coffee County Court in Manchester for trial on the criminal charge of giving a check for the sum of $800 in purchase of a commodity within the State of

Tennessee which was not honored on presentment. It turned out to be a capital offense punishable by 10 years in Tennessee prison. The truckdriver and his friends picked me up at my home in Niles and transported me personally to the trial. We drove all night and arrived at 8 a.m. I had the distinct feeling I was in custody and if the truckdriver did not come back, I would not either.

When I drive south to Florida now on Route 78, past Manchester, Tennessee, I am always tempted to revisit the old Courthouse which is centered in the Community with downtown buildings ranging about it on all sides.

The Courtroom was the kind of forum Clarence Darrow must have tried his Monkey case in. It was vintage 1850. There were spittoons by each counsel table, one by the judge's desk. An old oaken bucket filled with water had a ladle in it. Whenever anyone in the courtroom was thirsty, during recess, if they required a drink during trial session, the ladle was used to quench the person's thirst. Everyone but old Judge Smart and I had taken off his coat and was in shirt sleeves. The windows were open and flies buzzed about. It was hot and sticky, but I was determined to keep my coat on despite the heat. The attorney general was an expert at spitting. He made the mark in any spittoon he aimed for. Unfortunately for me during the proceedings before the jury that was empaneled— and I do think it was a deliberate act on his part to embarrass me and shake me in front of the jury — he would occasionally aim for the spittoon under the defense table.

There was no reporter, the case was to have no formal record maintained. In the event of an appeal, I was told by co-counsel that the attorneys recall of the events made up the record.

Old Judge Smart — he was at least 85 years of age — was to take a close, indeed to my view, a greatly biased overview of the entire proceedings. The Courtroom was crowded early in the morning. Obviously in this little country town in the middle of Tennessee in the '50's, the Courtroom was the main attraction. It had been well-rumored that an attorney from out of the state was going to represent some damnable foreigner who had given a check for $800 to one of the local potato farmers, had taken the potatoes out of the state and stopped payment on the check. Most of the crowd of spectators were potato growers. This was going to be quite a show.

I had retained a local lawyer, a tall Lincolnesque man in appearance, a former probate judge, but I was to handle the entire action.

Judge Smart personally called the session to order and the first item was his salty introduction of me to all assembled. "I want you to meet," said the judge, "a god-damned yankee lawyer from the State of Michigan. Now we are not going to allow him to be a foreigner long in these parts. So under the authority vested in me I declare him to be a Tennessee Colonel and hereafter he will be addressed as Colonel Keller."

I was shocked, nonplused, and grateful all in one emotion. It was soon evident everyone in the Courtroom had a title. My adversary, a huge, bare-chested hairy man — he worked in his open shirt and his chest was bare to his belly button — was an Assistant Attorney General of Tennessee. I suppose all prosecutors in Tennessee are called Assistant Attorney Generals. Throughout the trial he was addressed as General. My associate was Judge Moss. there was a Senator somebody. Of course I was addressed as Colonel Keller.

It was a strange proceeding. Something of the mould of a Kangaroo Court. There was no jury box and no very impartial pulling out of numbers to select the jury. The judge just asked if there were 12 men in the audience who would care to sit on the panel as jurors. As though by prearrangement, 12 men got up and came forward. Judge Moss was to *voir dire* them. Most of them were Coffee County potato growers. There were some challenges made but essentially we were to confront a jury panel, friendly to the local complainant, hostile to the Defendant. The case started about 8:30 a.m. and was to continue with trial breaks until 10 p.m. when the jury retired.

The burly Attorney General put on his case and he relished setting forth the proofs before the panel. This foreigner had bought U.S. #1 potatoes from the local grower and had given him a check for $800 which turned out to be dishonored and not paid. He went on to relate the complainant was a veteran of World War II and had been a potato grower in Coffee County, Tennessee, for 15 years. My Defendant testified from the stand he was a truckdriver who carried Michigan produce to Florida and enroute north back home had tried to pick up some Tennessee potatoes instead of "deadheading" or going back empty. The potatoes had been represented to him as U.S. Number One potatoes. They proved to be offgrade and commercial and not as represented. He had stopped payment only to protect his loss.

The Attorney General and I made our respective arguments to the jury, each of us obviously emphasizing our partisan feelings. I sensed the extreme partisan bias against the Defendant because of his being a northerner and I emphasized that three wars had succeeded the Civil War conflict and that Americans from both the north and south of the Mason Dixon Line had fought together and died in common cause for many years. These jurors should not sully their decision by ruling against the Defendant because some might say he was just a "damm yankee."

It was Judge Smart's instructions to the jury which most distressed me. "Now men of this jury, it is your duty to bring in a verdict which properly reflects the facts in this case. It is all well and easily said, as Colonel Keller has said it that his client was just trying to protect his loss when he stopped payment on this check. But I tell you, we have a statute in this state which protects our citizens from foreigners who come in here, take our produce, and when they leave our state, cancel their checks. A check given in this state is like currency and when given, it must be honored with no reservations. If you find the Defendant has violated the law of our State, you return a verdict of guilty and leave it to me to render the sentence."

I was disturbed. It had all the appearances of a very biased instruction to the jury, tilting them in effect to bring back a verdict of guilty. My Defendant and his truckdriver friends were dismayed. I was feeling the heat because it had been my advice which had placed the Defendant at peril. The jury retired at 6 o'clock and were excused for supper. They returned to their deliberations at 7 o'clock and were to remain out until 11 p.m. when they appeared before the Court. My client remained rigidly beside me as we all stood while the jury was arrayed. To the Court's call, that the foreman identify himself and announce the verdict, a tall rangy looking man, obviously a man of the soil, stood and announced: "We hang!"

The Defendant sagged and turned white. He didn't understand. I felt an intense relief for I was mentally resigned we were not going to receive an acquittal under these circumstances.

Old Judge Smart was apoplectic! The Court had been in session all day from 8:30 a.m. to 11 p.m. and the men on this jury had not shown the competence and rugged will to return a verdict in this case. This could not be allowed and the jury was instructed they must return a verdict and finish their duty regardless of the hour. He would not have it otherwise.

My relief now turned to dismay. My client and his buddies insisted on going to a bar at the edge of town and they insisted I stay and contact them when the jury returned. They confided to me they had no intention of the Defendant returning back to the Court should the jury return a verdict of guilty! They had lost confidence in Tennessee justice. I had no choice but to remain in the Courtroom alone awaiting the return of the jury I was very uncertain how I could handle the matter.

The jury did not return until 12:15 a.m. The Court asked for the appearance of my client and refused to allow the jury to announce its verdict until he appeared. I was ordered to produce him. I called the bar and was met by a friend of the Defendant who drove me to the tavern. I told my client the turn of events required his return with me. It was the only thing we could do. He and his friends believed the jury would announce a guilt verdict and the Defendant in no way was going to spend 10 years in a Tennessee prison. They were convinced Judge Smart was a hanging judge. I begged and pleaded with him he would never know the result and if he ran he would be a fugitive. Sometime after 1 a.m. he relented and came back with me to the Court. It took a lot of courage on his part.

The panel foreman again announced the jury was hopelessly deadlocked. The Attorney General announced he would move for retrial. After a quick consultation with my client, I announced we would pay the check. This we promptly did and the proceedings were terminated. I forfeited all claim to any fee. Enroute home with the truckers, and we left immediately, they confided that if their friend was to stay in Tennessee they weren't going to bring me back either. I never tried another case in Tennessee.

THE LIMA, OHIO STUNTFLYER WHO LOST HIS PASSENGER

A very interesting case was a criminal defense in Jennings County, Ohio, in the 1950's. One Bruce Overmeyer was involved and I was never paid a fee in this case, either. I should have written a story about it for publication but have told it many times and it has always amused my listeners. Bruce called me from jail in Lima, Ohio, early on a Monday morning. He was charged with manslaughter in the sky he said. I did not quite understand. He went on to relate that he had lost a passenger in his PT 19 World War II open seat trainer airplane, who fell to his death from a height of 2000 feet. Would I defend him? It sounded intriguing. It was not long before my wife Rachel and I journeyed to Lima, Ohio.

Bruce Overmeyer was a steeplejack and he loved high places. He owned a trainer plane which he kept out at the airport and he delighted in doing rolls, loops and maneuvers with it. One of his steeplejack ground crew members was an elderly man named George whose son was a local Lima Police Lieutenant. The old man was really a lonely old bum who had lost his wife and was abandoned by his kin. He hung around Bruce because he admired his work as a steeplejack. One Sunday the two of them went to a bar and managed to get well into their cups. It was getting on late in the afternoon and some time around 5 o'clock p.m. Bruce suggested to the old fellow that he might like going for a joy ride in the sky. George happily agreed.

The two of them made it out to the airport around 6 o'clock. When the airport manager saw them approach Bruce's plane, he was nettled. Closing time was at dusk as a rule and it was definitely approaching dusk. He wanted to close shop and go home. He suspected Bruce would perform some maneuvers in his plane and he was determined to call the police if he did. CAA Rules and Regulations provide that a pilot of any plane who performs acrobatics must provide his passenger with a parachute. An acrobatic is defined as any maneuver exceeding 20 degrees from parallel. The manager knew that Bruce had no parachutes in his plane. He assembled some 20 persons on the field and instructed them to alert him if Bruce's plane exceeded CAA Regulations. He would have Bruce cited if this happened.

In the meantime, not knowing he was being monitored, Bruce put his passenger in the rear seat, buckled him in, seated himself behind the controls in the front seat and took off. It wasn't long before the plane was 2000 feet high. Bruce signaled George he was going to do a loop. The old man showed his teeth in a happy grin. Around the clock past and over 12 o'clock the plane went. One of the ground observers broke free and ran to tell the airport manager that Bruce had executed a loop.

More was to follow. When Bruce brought the plane around he told George he was going to do it again. Again he revved up the plane and climbed to 9 o'clock, 10 o'clock and 11 o'clock. He couldn't get the plane over. The plane slid back on its tail and did a thunderhead stall! At the bottom of the slide, the nose went down sharply and the tail whipped up. Poor George flew out of the plane and fell headlong to earth. The group of watchers below were shocked. One of the observers ran to tell the manager while the others watched stunned as the plane leveled out and its pilot brought it in to land.

After the thunderhead stall, Bruce looked back to see George and was nonplused to find the seat empty. He was in somewhat of a stupor state and he had trouble remembering if he had put him in the seat and buckled him in. He landed the plane and jumped on the wing before getting off and examined the seat. The buckle was undone, the straps were opened. He stumbled off without so much as a greeting to the shocked personnel standing in the field, got into his car and drove to the premises where he was shacked up with a woman, not his wife. He told her he was in some kind of trouble. He did not have long to wait. The airport manager called the Sheriff and they took Bruce into custody. It was from the jail he had called me the following morning. He had at one time lived in Niles and knew me.

Such were the facts of the case. The prosecutor had issued a warrant charging reckless homicide. There was a highway statute describing reckless homicide involving a motor vehicle. He simply fashioned from this statute the complaint against Bruce alleging that in violation of the Civil Aeronautics Authority regulations, Bruce had recklessly carried aloft a passenger unequipped with a parachute and performed an acrobatic maneuver.

I went out to the airfield in advance of the trial and talked to the manager. One question bothered me and somehow I thought it was going to be crucial. I inquired of the manager the names of all the witnesses and interviewed them. Had anyone heard the passenger scream when he fell helplessly? None had. The manager scoffed at my inquiry. I couldn't know much about airplanes. Had I ever flown? Yes, in commercial planes. No one could hear a scream from a plane 500 feet high, let alone 2000 feet high. I did not believe that and I proposed to him, knowing he was going to be a key prosecution witness, that we conduct an experiment. Let's put up a Piper Cub airplane at 500 feet, 1000 feet, 1500 feet and finally 2000 feet, have the pilot yell at the top of his lungs and the two of us on the field below would judge if the scream could be heard. He agreed. So it was arranged that a young pilot take up a Piper Cub plane to these elevations consecutively and yell at the top of his lungs. The manager and I stood on the ground, ears cupped. The yell at 500 feet was piercingly clear. Very audible at 1000 feet and 1500 feet. At 2000 feet over the roar of an approaching plane, the scream of the pilot was audible to us. The manager agreed that he was wrong. A body falling from 2000 feet high emitting a scream of terror could be heard below by personnel listening on the ground!

A lawyer must plan his strategy for the trial in advance of the hearing. He cannot, certainly in a case where the adversary has strong proofs, hope blindly that his mere monitoring presence in the proceedings will suffice to serve the client's cause. The prosecutor's proofs in this case were going to be impressive. It was not going to be an easy defense.

The prosecutor was a young man who had studied for the ministry. He had a large number of witnesses, including the airport manager, several of his ground observers that he had instructed to watch the plane, a police lieutenant who turned out to be the deceased's son, friends of the deceased, employees of the bar which served booze to George, and finally an aviation expert of some sort who was to testify the application of the CAA Regulations restricting acrobatics. I could not recall having any other witness to present than the Defendant Bruce Overmeyer.

I was going to have to make out our defense proofs by cross-examination of the prosecution's witnesses! These witnesses followed in a literal parade. The old man's son, a police officer who, unobserved by me, carried onto the stand his service revolver, admitted his father was a lonely and often bitter old man who seldom visited family or friends. My cross-examination of the officer was critical. It had been developed by a witness that George had, on one occasion, been in a crowd gathered about a third story window from which a would-be-suicide threatened to jump. George had muttered something to the effect that if he ever jumped he would want to jump from a higher than third floor level.

I may very well have angered the officer by querying him on. His father's habits, the hopelessness of his circumstances, his despondency and lack of interest in people, including family about him, were not pleasant for him to recall. My wife Rachel in the audience observed the gun and pointed it out during recess. When the trial resumed the officer took his stand again, and, in the presence of the jury, I insisted he disarm himself before I continued examination of him.

The people of the field who had observed the horrible accident testified to seeing the old man fall or jump from the plane after it had stalled going into the attempted loop at a distance of approximately 2000 feet high from the ground. No one had heard him scream or yell as he plummeted towards earth. Finally the CAA regulation providing for the prohibition of any acrobatic maneuver if the passenger was not provided a parachute was introduced in evidence.

The critical witness was the airport manager. As he was carried through his direct examination by the prosecutor, it was evident that the latter knew nothing of my prior contact with the man. On my cross-examination, the manager admitted I had interviewed him at the airport. He had scoffed at my suggestion a scream, if emitted, could be heard in the ground from a plane 2000 feet high, or even 500 feet high. We had watched the test plane go up consecutively to the levels of 500 feet, 1000 feet, 1500 feet, and finally 2000 feet elevation and we could both hear the pilot scream. He agreed that at the last height, though faint over the roar of another airplane, the scream was audible at ground level.

Bruce Overmeyer's testimony was critical but not wholly helpful. He felt sorry for the old man and related how they had spent the Sunday afternoon together, finally going out to the airport and getting into the plane. Importantly, he was certain that he had solidly buckled the old man into the seat before going up. After the incident when he landed the plane he detailed how the belt was unbuckled and the belt straps lay open on the seat. He was cross-examined critically on the way he was living. He had left his wife and three children and had shacked up with another woman. He wasn't an attractive fellow who was going to win any sympathy from the jury.

By the time arguments were scheduled, the courtroom was tense.

My wife in the audience was seated beside a woman who identified herself as the Judge's wife. The Judge had told her some hot shot from Michigan was the attorney for the defense and it was an interesting criminal case and suggested she come. I knew all depended on the defense argument.

My argument was centered on the opened safety belt which Bruce Overmeyer had testified he observed after landing the plane:

"Ladies and gentlemen, this poor old man was a lonely forlorn derelict. Nobody was paying any attention to him but the Defendant. He had witnessed suicides who jumped out of buildings. Doubtless he had said to himself if ever he jumped to his death he wanted to do it from higher than a third floor ledge. They would have to pick him up in a basket. Put yourself in his mood and frame of mind. You are 2000 feet high, a sense of freedom and repose suffuses you and your senses. Bruce had signaled a loop and what an excitement it was. The loop was completed and Bruce signaled he was going to do a second loop. The thought comes to you what an easy and pleasant way to go. The first thing to do is unbuckle the safety belt and then jump or fall out. You unbuckle the belt. Then it happens! You are freefalling in space 2000 feet high and there is no getting back now and you are hurtling earthward to your final doom. Jury members! If you had intended to fall or jump out, you would have gone silently without a whimpering moan or word. This was the relief you had prayed for many times in a lonely life which had ceased to have any meaning for you. Your descent would be a silent one.

"If you had no will or intention to jump or fall out and had accidentally been flung free from the plane, you would have been terrified. You would have screamed in horror like a banshee, all the way until your violent impact with mother earth stilled your voice forever. Ladies and gentlemen! The old man went to his death silently. Ho one heard any scream of terror or shout flung out by the figure plummeting earthward. This was no homicide attributable to the Defendant. This was suicide!"

The jury returned a verdict of not guilty in the case of the lost passenger, "Was He Suicide or Homicide?" as was the widely reported version in the area. On reflection, it was the only real issue in the action. Some may urge that a man flung out of a plane would be terrified speechless. I don't recall the prosecutor urged that position. It may be, but my thesis was at least arguable. The jury, hearing all of the facts, believed that the old man himself had terminated his life. Mr. Overmeyer was simply the vehicle for that act of self-destruction.

WYCKO VS. GNODTKE: THE CHILD DEATH CASE THAT CHANGED THE LAW OF DAMAGES

I frequently was asked, as other attorneys had often done, to talk to high school students about law as a profession. A priceless heritage of our democratic society is the right to an open trial. I told the students and I meant every word of it, there was no more thrilling experience than to be able to throw open the doors of the Courtroom and there defend and advance the rights and the cause of action of an individual. Jury duty must be regarded a privilege to serve and participate in the democratic way of life. The jury members must feel confidence in the integrity of the lawyer, representing his client, or they cannot relate well to the client's cause. I told them the most satisfying aspect of the career of a trial lawyer was the satisfaction of standing and helping someone in a crisis.

The supreme thrill was to wrestle with the law insofar as it was archaic and ill-served society, and to participate in making law a better vehicle to serve mankind in the modern world. I pointed out there were many areas in tort negligence law where ancient legal precedents were impediments to the attainment of full justice today. The ideal of striving on principle to make the law mirror the needs of present day society and serve its needs should be a stimulating motivation encouraging students to study law. The students reacted affirmatively. A few of them later told me they were inspired to enter the profession.

The case which exemplified my ambition to pioneer in the law and advance a landmark precedent to fully obtain justice in the personal injury area was the case of Wycko vs. Gnodtke, 105 NW2d 118, 361 Mich 331, which reached the Supreme Court of Michigan in September, 1960. That case has been acclaimed by many scholars and practicing attorneys as one of the most important landmark cases in the State of Michigan and indeed in the country. Before Wycko, a concept of damages for the death of a negligently killed child prevailed which in no way mirrored the society of the mid-20th Century. The old rule of damages was a peculiarly archaic child labor standard which aped a culture more akin to the Middle Ages. It left attorneys in that era very perplexed precisely how to make any sensible claim for damages suffered by grieving parents for the loss of a negligently killed child.

In the 1950's, the Michigan Statute providing for wrongful death had been little, if any, changed since 1848 when it was first put in force. It was modeled after the "Lord Campbell Statute" in England which first gave remedy sounding in damages for the wrongful death of another. In common law there was no remedy. The Michigan Statute provided that in a wrongful death action, if negligence was proven, the Court instruct the jury to give such damages as were deemed fair and just with reference to the "pecuniary injury resulting from such death" to those persons entitled to same. For the negligently slain husband or wife, the surviving spouse or kin could bring suit against the tortfeasor who had caused such death, at least for the loss of support of the deceased husband (and/or father) or services of the deceased wife (and/or mother). Even in the latter instance, the surviving spouse or kin had to wrestle with the numbing "worth" of a good wife. The cost of a substitute house-keeper, a cleaning woman, a baby-sitter and other personnel required to provide the services of a deceased wife (or mother) was a clumsy yard-stick to measure damage loss, but at least it was available.

In the case of a slain child in his minority, the statutory measure of damages, namely "pecuniary loss," was the only measure the law recognized as recovery for wrongful death damages. The statute pro-vided no relief. A child in modern society is a burden, withal a blessed one, not usually a source of profit for services comporting with the statu-tory term "pecuniary." The problem therefore of recovering damages for the wrongful death of a child was a very difficult one for the Plaintiff's lawyer. In the great majority of states, including Michigan, where the pecuniary measure was the statutory rule, the attorney was unaided by the Lord Campbell type of wrongful death statute which provided for damages only for pecuniary loss or pecuniary injury resulting from such death. When cases for damages for the wrongful death of a child were in fact brought in that era, the Court was bound to instruct the jury, pursu-ant to the statute, damages must be limited to the amount of money the parent could reasonably be expected to receive from the child's earn-ings, <u>had he continued to live between the date of his death and his 21st birthday, which was the age of his majority, less the amount of support, nurture and care the parent would have given his child during that pe-riod.</u> This was a concept of the child's value to his parent out of context with the way we reared our families in the 20th century. Instead, it was tuned to the Dickens era, long before child labor laws, when a child's worth was measured by the shekels he earned at the mill or factory and brought home to his family to somehow offset his "care and keep." In the 20th century we have child labor laws to protect our children from being exploited as chattel, bred for hire, and we pour into their upbring-ing a host of creature comforts, educational opportunities, medical at-tention, in addition to mere housing and food costs, all designed to ma-ture, educate and render them useful citizens, and promote their matu-rity. Furthest from the mind of the parent is the concept of exploiting them as the Court's charge suggested. Juries had trouble adapting to the charge when made and they must have oft listened in amazement to the trial court instruction which deliberately charged them to adapt their verdict to a child labor standard.

In the case of Courtney vs. Appel, 76NW2d 80, 345 Mich 223, a jury receiving that instruction, returned a verdict of $700 for the burial expenses, nothing for the child. In that case, the Courtney boy, age 3, had been killed by a negligent automobile driver and the parent brought suit for death damages.

The jury's response of no damages for the child's death was a forthright response to the Court's statutory instruction of double-entry bookkeeping based on the child labor formula. Circuit Court Judge Eugene Black, later to be elevated to the Supreme Court of Michigan, was shocked and revolted, and on his independent motion, directed a new trial on damages only. The defense, delighted with the verdict, appealed to the Supreme Court seeking to reinstate the jury verdict. The Supreme Court did just that with its majority decision. Justice Talbot Smith, an illustrious jurist whose decisions in the late '50's, '60's, and '70's were thrilling, challenging and always highly literate prose, pinpointing with sure feeling the excision of many archaic postures of the law and compelling by their sheer logic the upgrading of precedents to modern needs, wrote for reversal in a surefire dissenting opinion.

For the jury function I have a profound respect. That, plus the inexorable logic of my Brother's opinion, led me to a tentative acceptance thereof. But the case would not leave me. My misgivings first arose with the thought that if this had been a prize bull, negligently killed on the highway without negligence on the part of its owner, the owner could have collected his full damages. But with respect to this little boy negligently killed on the highway, without negligence on the part of his parents, a jury verdict that the father is entitled to no damages is permitted to stand undisturbed by us. I recoil from the comparison, but I recoil even more from the result. It is not the law of this jurisdiction that a negligent killer of a healthy little three-year old boy will be permitted to walk scot-free from any court to which runneth our writ.

The jurist then reviewed the entire history of the Lord Campbell's Act type of statutory remedy of damages limited to pecuniary loss and his ultimate position was that a parent is entitled to a substantial award and the jury should be unequivocally somehow instructed to give it. Justice Black was eminently correct in ordering a new trial on damages only. Justice Black by this time had been elevated to the Supreme Court but took no part in the Courtney decision.

The Courtney case came to be known as the "Worthless Child Case," throughout Michigan and throughout the country. Michigan Lawyers came to know that if an appropriate child death damage suit were to be appealed to the Supreme Court, Justice Talbot Smith at least was ready to address it and the Michigan "pecuniary value" statute forthrightly. Shortly there were other liberal-minded jurists on the bench, notably Justice Black himself and others who would join with Justice Smith. The temper of the Court was changing.

An ATLA Seminar on wrongful death was chaired by an attorney named William Beal in Cincinnati, Ohio, in 1957 or 1958. I attended because I was interested. The Courtney "Worthless Child Case" was discussed. These were Plaintiffs attorneys gathering to exchange their views and encourage one another to mount an assault on the archaic concept of pecuniary value damages in wrongful child death actions. Craig Spangenberg, a brilliant lawyer from Cincinnati and frequent contributor to seminars, spoke on substituting possibly a lost investment rule for the child labor formula of services less upkeep. It seemed plausible for investment related to the concept of pecuniary. Sympathy, bereavement, solatium and loss of companionship appeared barred by the statutory standard. I came away from the seminar inspired.

It was not long thereafter I was to be drawn into the challenge. John Wycko and his wife were the parents of three boys. One had died in an automobile accident in Chicago. John determined to move his family to a rural, more safe area and he brought them to a farm in Sawyer, a little country town in Berrien County, Michigan. John was a salesman and he believed his family safe on the farm when he was away. His concern for his family should have been soundly assured. It was to prove otherwise to the devastation of husband and wife.

The two Wycko boys, one aged 12 and the other (John L. Wycko, Jr.), aged 14, were members of a Boy Scout Troop. One night after the troop meeting had terminated, the troop and column of boys wound their way along and completely off the east side of a road near Sawyer, to their respective homes. As the boys in the column approached their homes, they would peel off and leave the column until it was finally reduced to 5 lads, the two Wycko boys in the middle.

Armond Gnodtke, a young man of approximately 17 years, was driving his father's car northbound on that road. Somehow his attention was diverted from the highway ahead of him and he drove off the road into the center of the Boy Scout column, killing the two Wycko boys. Gnodtke fled the scene of the accident but later turned himself in. It was an open and shut case of liability!

The Wyckos were devastated by their grief. They sought and secured the services of Lawyer Theron Childs in Three Oaks, Michigan. Childs practiced probate and corporation law, primarily. He was ultimately to advise the Wyckos that the insurance adjuster for the Gnodtkes had made a maximum offer of $1,500 per child, namely $1,000 for the funeral expenses and $500 for each child, a total of $3,000 for the two sons. He explained to them the limitation of the pecuniary rule of damages in child death cases under the statute. They were not in any way satisfied and indeed their grief was exacerbated by the insult of the proffered settlement. I received a call one day at my office in Niles from the Wyckos.

The Wyckos wanted my services. I was intrigued with the challenge of the case for I recognized its potential immediately. Here was a magnificent opportunity to challenge and wrestle with the law to make it more adequately serve a tragic modern social problem. How can one best measure in dollars the damage loss of a negligently killed child? There were many arguing, and lawyers and judges were among them, that money damages somehow vulgarized the human loss and should not be attempted. Their thesis was that grief and loss of companionship could simply not be related to money compensation. I strongly felt a different composure. Justice Smith's onfire dissent in the Courtney case and the Worthless Child discussions at the Cincinnati seminar had kindled a compelling interest on my part, given the proper case, to do something to struggle for a change in the law.

I told the Wyckos I would meet them for dinner at the Whitcomb Hotel in St. Joseph, Michigan. They were a simple, unassuming and very likable couple. Tremendously saddened by the loss of all of their children, they were also very upset by the paltry sum offered them in settlement for their two boys. I explained I should feel privileged to represent them in the trial of their causes of action and would not entertain any settlement. I explained the statute, the Courtney case dissent, and my feeling that the statutory definition of pecuniary loss ought to be challenged by an appeal all the way to the Supreme court. I remember telling them that the action thus carried might very well come to be a fitting memorial for their deceased boys. Their interest seemed sparked by the suggestion. I told them I should require Attorney Childs' consent to participate with me jointly in such action as I did not wish to replace him. I was not interested in taking another lawyer's file from him. They agreed. I was to call Childs and tell him what I proposed to do. I would commence one action only and that for the 14 year old boy, John Wycko, Jr., try to make new law for damages and then trying the other action when that law was established, hopefully within the term of the limitation period. He was noncommittal and not particularly enthused. I told him I would do all the trial preparation and work and the expected appeal and split directly with him the fee. This generous offer on my part was an abundantly fair proposal which he accepted. He was to appear of counsel with me on the trial level and on appeal but I alone was to be responsible for the action.

Suit was commenced for the one boy only. I knew I had to create error early in the case else there would be no appeal issue and I had no illusions. I had to make the law of the case in novel context. I had written and carried on some extensive correspondence with Thomas Lambert, erudite Editor-in-Chief of the ATLA law journal, successor to the venerable Harvard Law School Dean Pound, a professor of law at Suffolk Law School, Boston, Massachusetts. Lambert was one of Justice Jackson's principal assistant prosecutors in the Nuremberg trials and a remarkable lawyer whose addresses were eagerly attended by lawyers all over the country. I expressed to him my thoughts about the case.

Lambert and I were to exchange correspondence throughout the case and he was to encourage me on. "The acorn you plant now," he wrote me, "will a mighty oak grow."

As soon as the jury was empaneled and before the presentation of any proofs, I submitted to trial Judge Thomas Robinson a requested allowance for the following instruction taking the position that my proofs would be substantially affected by the allowance or rejection of same:

"If you find from the evidence that the Defendant Armond Gnodtke was guilty of negligence causing the death of Plaintiff's minor son and that the latter was not guilty of contributory negligence as I have defined those terms to you, and you therefore find that the Defendants, Armond Gnodtke and Emil Gnodtke are liable for the Plaintiff minor's death, you are instructed by the Court that in arriving at a determination of the pecuniary loss to the parents (which the statute refers to) the result of the killing of their son, you may take into consideration and employ as a yardstick or measure of damages, the investment of the parents in their child from the time of his birth including prenatal, hospitalization and medical care of confinement, through infancy and schooling up to the time of his death, including funeral expenses.
"Take into consideration all of their costs and expenses connected with this young man — medical, food, shelter, schooling and instructional — from birth, thru school, to death, in arriving at your determination of the total investment of the

parents in their son up to the time of his death. Your verdict should determine this computed total investment as the dollar and cents replacement value of the boy and you will thereby arrive at the pecuniary loss to the parents the result of the death of their son.

"One who injures another by his negligent act must, under our laws, respond in damages for that injury and the only way that damages can be ordered in our society is in terms of money retribution. Life cannot be restored but this is not to say that life has no value and a mortal jury must not shrink from the assessment of that value. You are therefore to consider the investment of these parents and the dollar and cents costs of the replacement of that investment in their son to the time of his death as the measure of their pecuniary loss.

"The law presumes the life of a minor child to be of value to his parents, who are necessarily injured by a wrongful act resulting in his death. To compensate the parents for this injury and loss the law allows substantial damages and these damages may be measured by the experience and judgment of the jury in these matters, enlightened by a knowledge of the age, sex and condition in life of the deceased child. The parents are not restricted to the recovery of merely nominal damages, just because the details of their investment in their son, even unto the funeral expenses, be not proven. As jurors, you have the right to draw from your common observation in matters of this nature and determine approximately what amount will compensate the death of their minor son.

"If you find such loss to the parents resulted solely from the wrongful acts of the Defendant Armond Gnodtke, then I charge you that such proof as has been furnished in this case is sufficient to authorize an award for substantial damages."

Judge Robinson's reaction was prompt, classic and patently final for trial purposes:

"The Court has not given very much consideration to your request, because the Court hasn't heard your opening statement, hasn't heard the proofs; and the Court is not going to give consideration to the question of instructions until in the due course of the trial at the proper time those considerations become important. The Court will indicate he does not intend to give such instruction as you started to expatiate. The court intends to follow the law as it is on the books, the statutes and the decisions of the Supreme Court of Michigan as they exist. The court is not expecting to pioneer in this case and make new law, if that is what you are seeking: for you must take the law as it is, and the court expects to take it as it is, not as you would like to have it or as the court might like to have it."

The rigid statutory pecuniary standard of damages to which I now was limited by the Court's refusal to accept my proposed instructions required that I put on testimony relating to the farm labors of the young lad on his father's 10 acre farm such as picking berries and similar jobs, and the many tasks and chores which a farm boy would perform, all done prior to his death. Thereby I sought to somehow establish his speculative value to his parents from death date to 21 years when he would be literally emancipated. All this had to be reduced by the cost of his keep during that period. Proofs were strained as indeed they had to be under the pecuniary value standard of the statute then existing. I knew, the defense knew and the court knew there was no way that a sum of any substance sounding in damages for the loss of a child's life was going to muster acceptance by a jury which followed the expected Court instruction.

Something very interesting occurred in Court chambers during the trial and before argument. My declaration had asked the sum in damages of $30,000 for the lost boy, John Wycko, Jr. The judge knew that many times juries had given me precisely my demand to the penny and he inquired of me how much I would actually ask of the jury in argument. He commented that he would certainly not let stand any verdict of $30,000. "How about $20,000?" I asked the judge. He would not abide

$20,000. I persisted. "How about $10,000?" The judge said he would allow a $10,000 award. I then proposed $15,000. Judge Robinson said he did not know about $15,000 and I remarked that I would ask $15,000. My demand to the jury was for $14,000 plus $979.50 for the burial expenses.

In argument to the jury, I threw caution to the winds and I launched an impassioned plea to the panel that in fantasy they walk with me beside the bier of the little 14 year old deceased Wycko boy, look at his corpse and tell me that damages to his parents for his loss was limited by the wholly speculative and limited pecuniary value of his services to his parents, less keep, had he lived from death to emancipation at age 21. I dared them to answer me that the parents had suffered no loss the result of their boy's death. If any one of that jury could do that they should be consistent and award to the negligent tortfeasor an award for removing the burden of a child's support from the grieving parents.

Attorney Dalton Seymour angrily rose to complain and object that I was impermissibly arguing the law. I was doing just that. Seymour knew it and Judge Robinson knew it. The Judge, who had been raptly following me, made comment that he was intrigued by my oratory and he invited Seymour to respond oratorically as well. The floor was now mine to use without further interruption and I made the most of it. I compared the 14 year old boy to a 14 year old sapling pine tree. I could have compared him to a prize young bull in the context of Justice Talbot Smith's dissent in the Courtney case. I did not. Every year the parents had expended money in raising their child from the time of his birth until his death, all to make a useful, good, mature and socially involved citizen of him, hopefully to become a source of support and solace in their old age. I told them of the medical care, the support and the training, including violin lessons they had within their means lavished on him and their hopes for his ultimate mature success. Here were no parents interested in the taking away of his earnings in the manner of a double-entry accounting column of services less keep. They did not seek to profit from him as they would a chattel or a slave. This was a loved child and I invited the jury to come into the 20th century and leave the era of the middle ages of England when a child earned his pittance in the mill and this was his only worth. If they could not do that and they were able to follow the Court's Child Labor formula and award nothing to the parents for the loss of their child, they should rationally be able to award, on a counterclaim, a verdict to the Defendant for a substantial sum of money, all for removing the burden of raising a child from the back of the grieving parents. We did not ask any sympathy from them for our grief and loss. We did not want one penny of sympathy, but we did want and required damages for the very real injury the parents had suffered. I pointed out figuratively the pine tree, raised, nurtured, fed and fertilized for 14 years to its fine growth and then destroyed carelessly by the act of another. The owner of the destroyed tree surely could successfully claim the value of his investment in that tree from planting to growth and destruction, all from the person responsible for its destruction. I concluded by asking a minimum of $1,000 per year for the investment of the parents in the child from date of his birth to his death. We justly required at least $1,000 per year for the cost of the parent's investment for their child from birth to death, now lost irretrievably. At least this was an easily recognized loss to the parents for the child's death. If the wrongdoer had broken out a window, at minimum he should be compelled to restore the broken glass. The jury could not restore the child's life, but at least it should award the parents their loss of investment in the child. Anything less would be monstrous. Adding the funeral bill of $979.50, I demanded return of a verdict of $14,979.50. The jury listened intently and the verdict was in sum precisely my demand.

I was not happy with the result! I had received everything I had asked for from the jury. The loss of investment plus funeral charges. But where was my appeal issue? What lasting import was such a verdict by a Circuit Court jury going to have on the law itself?

The defense, fortunately for me, would not let the verdict lie. Defense counsel asked for a new trial on the ground the verdict of $14,000 was excessive. Judge Robinson, now confronted with a $15,000 verdict which earlier he said would leave him with uncertain resolve, ruled that unless I voluntarily took a remitter or reduction to $8,479.50 ($7,500 plus $979.50) he would order a retrial. No boy of 14 years of age, he ruled, was worth to his parents from that age until he arrived at 21, any sum in excess of $7,500 under the child labor formula, unless he were of unusual means and capacity which was not shown in this case. In Court I thanked the Judge and said I would appeal, which I did.

I will always believe Judge Robinson saved the case for appeal deliberately and I am indebted to him for the position he took. He was to become seriously ill and expire October 8, 1960. I left him with a copy of the slip opinion of the Supreme Court when I received it and it was found among his effects at the hospital when he expired. I know he was as thrilled as I with Justice Talbot Smith's opinion.

My argument to the Supreme Court, both by brief and orally was concise and to the point:

I urged the Supreme Court of Michigan to restore the jury award for the Wycko boy, but more important, that it overrule Courtney vs. Appel and bring Michigan out of the Middle Ages child labor formula which required the application of a measure of damages for a wrongfully killed child based on the value of the child's services fictionally from date of death to age of emancipation, less cost of keep. That formula, I argued, was consistent with a bygone era when children were raised by parents as chattel and early put in the mill or factory to earn their keep. The concept of rearing children for hire and profit came right out of Dickens' time. In no way did it mirror the way parents raised their children to maturity in the mid 20th century. So out of context with our society was it that the law, which must serve as an instrument to serve human needs, was demeaned. Parents who reared their children to useful, mature human beings and never benefited from them financially, must be revolted by the worthless child formula and I asked that it be, root and branch, removed and abolished.

Dalton Seymour never understood why I refused, at any time during or after trial, or appeal before the Supreme Court decision, to discuss settlement at any level for the Wycko cases, singularly or for the two of them. I said I was simply not interested in any money offer and discouraged any negotiation. He was understandably critical of my stance and said I had no right as a lawyer to refuse negotiations. I was solely concerned with changing the law and felt that was a higher goal than earning a fee. Importantly, I had my clients' full consent for that posture. Indeed that was an understood and explicit condition of my retainer.

Justice Talbot Smith, known widely for his brilliant opinions on the bench, was a jewel on the finest Michigan Supreme Court bench assembled since the days of Justice Cooley. He must have regarded the Wycko case as the answer to his on fire dissent in Courtney vs. Appel. Justices Black, Edwards, Cavanaugh, and Souris, concurred with him. Eugene Black was the trial judge in the trial of Courtney vs. Appel, who on his own motion had ordered new trial limited to damages for the death of the six year old boy. That case was, in part, the genesis of Wycko.

Justice Smith had no problem including the parents' lost investment in the child from birthdate to deathdate, which I had championed at trial level, as an element of pecuniary loss under the statute. He went well beyond that. The Justice exorcised the barbarous concept of the pecuniary loss to a parent from the death of the child based on the child labor formula as a reproach to justice and he solemnly declared that fiction employed as the measure of pecuniary loss should be forever abandoned. Thereby in one stroke the Circuit Court instructions to the jury involving the double-entry cost approach for damages for the death of a child, an instruction which had been employed for 100 years, was forever excised from Michigan law. Justice Smith's opinion went on to declare that the pecuniary value of a human life was a compound of many elements. He analogized human life with an industrial plant. Just as an item of machinery performing part of a functioning industrial plant had a value over and above that of a similar item in a showroom, so an individual member of the family has a value to others as a part of a functioning social and economic unit. That value, he said, is the value of mutual society and protection, mainly companionship. "The human companionship thus afforded has a definite, substantial and ascertainable pecuniary value and its loss forms a part of the 'value' of the life sought to be ascertained. Loss of companionship thereby is a viable element of the damages, call it pecuniary or otherwise, that a parent suffered when a child was taken from him" (Wycko vs.Gnodtke, 361 Mich Reports 331).

While appeal was pending prior to its publication, I was invited to address the issue of child death damages at the Mel Belli Seminar in San Francisco. The Wycko Supreme Court decision was hailed nation-wide. Professor Thomas Lambert, Editor-in-Chief of the ATLA law journal was enthusiastic in his praise of it. Wycko, he said, removed a blemish from the face of justice. He was to tell me that it was the subject of over 30 leading articles in leading law journals throughout the country. The decision was acclaimed throughout the state and indeed the nation as a great landmark case, and indeed it was, because it included loss of companionship as an element of damages, even under the pecuniary loss standard of the statute. It was to make possible successful argument for loss of companionship in wrongful death cases of not only children, but adults generally. It was to give a whole new dimension to damages in these cases. The day of the worthless child, the questionable value of the housewife, even the supporting husband, who was killed, all of this ceased to exist. No longer were such considerations to suppress the adequate valuation of these death claims. Plaintiffs' awards in these death cases were to remarkably increase in amount. I was called on to address seminars in death action cases throughout the state.

For a period of some ten years in the '60's, the Michigan Supreme Court was rocked by dissents and angry recriminations by one segment of the Court against the other. Justice Black who had sided with Justice Smith was to desert the liberal wing and swing over to the other side. It was his *sua sponte* order calling for a new trial on damages in the Courtney case when he was Circuit Judge that had sparked the appeal and spirited dissent of Justice Smith in the Courtney case. I never could understand his abandonment of the new damage approach to child death cases. His opinions were always brilliant and couched in no-nonsense, almost telegraphed-succinct prose and a professorially correct approach which permitted no equivocation of meaning or intent. I regarded him as one of the most astute, competent and erudite members of the bench. He was not easy on his fellows, often scathingly criticizing their opinions if they took a different tack than he. He was not popular with his colleagues. Essentially, his was an unfettered spirit.

One day in my Niles office, I received a personal call from Lansing. It was from Justice Eugene Black. We talked like old high school colleagues for over a half hour. The Justice said he was confronting an opinion he had to write in a case involving Wycko. Wasn't it true, he asked me, that I had only been interested in restoring the jury verdict of $15,000? A verdict of that size would seem to justify the old jury charge of double-entry accounting required by the child labor formula by the Court under the pecuniary value standard of the statute.

He had no trouble reconciling his assent to Justice Smith's controlling opinion in Wycko, but now years later he was troubled that the Wycko decision had impermissibly enlarged judicially the statutory standard. In his view the statute was going to be amended and that should be done by the legislature and not by the Court. He opined, this should have been left to legislative enactment and not judicial pronouncement. I was taken aback. No, I told him, I fully intended an assault on a judicial interpretation which reinforced a wholly archaic legislative mandate which did not reflect or serve our modern society. I agreed that I had not urged loss of companionship as an element of loss having pecuniary value, but I earnestly had proposed lost investment as an element, both before the jury and the Supreme Court in order to make the statute meaningful to our people. I was wholly in favor of Justice Talbot Smith's injection of the loss of companionship as an element of pecuniary value though I did concede that I had not personally had the courage to advance that approach. I reminded him of his good jurist posture as trial judge in the Courtney case and he expressed surprise that I should remember the case. He surely must have been revolted by the sure-fire rationale and logic of a jury panel in Courtney which, responding to the double-entry accounting formula of value of services less upkeep, had returned a verdict of zero damages for the death of the child. Why else had he *sua sponte* ordered retrial? Our conversation did not convince either of us the other's views. It was no surprise to me that in 1970 in the case of <u>Breckon vs. Franklin Fuel</u>, 383 Mich 251, Justice J. Black wrote the majority opinion reversing Wycko.

The reversal was not long to stand. In the cause of <u>Smith vs. City of Detroit</u>, 388 Mich 637, Wycko was reinstated and Breckon was overruled.

Not long thereafter the statute was legislatively amended, (PA65 effective 3/30/72), incorporating the Wycko element of loss of companionship for the surviving kin and damages for the wrongful death of anyone. Michigan had arrived in the 20th century. It is interesting to note that surrounding states of Indiana and Illinois still have the old pecuniary loss yardstick at arriving at wrongful death damages as do the States of New York and Pennsylvania. Lawyers in those states have to tussle with that old yardstick as we in Michigan prior to 1960.

I had contributed a remarkable new legal precedent in damage suits. I was the only Michigan member at the time of the New York State Trial Lawyers Association and traveled with them on their seminars over the world. The Wycko case was a stellar citation. I was many times requested to speak about it and soon it came to be when I would appear at conventions I was introduced and referred to as "Mr. Wycko."

APPLYING THE WYCKO DOCTRINE

Getting back to Wycko, in 1975, I was to employ the Wycko precedent in addressing wrongful death damages claims of the parents and the brothers of 12 year old Tracey Heater who had been fatally crushed when a free-standing book-loaded library shelf in the Hartford School System (Cass County, Michigan) had fallen over on her. I sat down with the family at a dinner in their home and tried to become a part of the family by spending the late afternoon and evening with them. I wanted to feel the sense of loss all of them had experienced in the death of an only daughter and only sister. It was important to me to literally crawl into their skins in order to sense that loss. I was mindful of Justice Smith's eloquent analysis of the value of each member to other members of the family unit and I wanted to be able to convey to the jury this sense of loss of both the parents and the brothers. The third day through trial in Paw Paw, Michigan, the defense attorney, himself the father of one girl and two boys, and sensitive to the loss suffered by the family, finally agreed to a consent judgement awarding damages of $100,000 to the parents, and $25,000 to the brothers for the loss of companionship of their only daughter and sister respectively. For me, Wycko had come full circle!

THE "ANATOMY OF A RAPE" CASE

An amusing incident occurred while with the New York group. I was asked if I had ever tried a case in the Marquette County Circuit Court, the scene of the "Anatomy of A Murder" movie starring Jimmy Stewart as a defense attorney and Congressman Welch as the trial judge. Justice Volkers of the Michigan Supreme Court, writing under the pen name John Travers had authored the book, a bestseller, and sold the script to Goldwyn-Mayer, which produced the enormously popular movie. To my questioner's disappointment, I had never tried a case in Marquette County.

It seemed Marquette was the only Court area in Michigan with which New York lawyers were familiar. Somehow the germ of an idea that I should try a case there took root. I was requested by the State Bar to address an UpperPeninsula Law Seminar in Escanaba, Michigan. The Upper Peninsula bar members are known to be a breed apart. They are an independent sort and practice law as a hobby, and are known to not let it interfere with their pursuit of hunting or fishing. At least that was the situation in the '60's. They were also generous to a fault and known to offer any Southern Michigan trial lawyer who lectured them participation in one of their trials to test his mettle. The invitation had attached to it an aura of excitement for any trial advocate and it was rumored that Bill Buchanan and Harold Sawyer, both eminent trial lawyers in the Grand Rapids area, had on their lecture tours accepted such invitations.

My subject at Escanaba was "Trial Strategy in the '60's" and I talked of Wycko and its challenge. Sure enough I had several offers of co-counseling offered me, one from an attorney in Iron Mountain, I believe the home of one of the Supreme Court Justices. Another such offer particularly intrigued me.

An attorney in Marquette had been retained by a Defendant charged with rape. The girl was pregnant and he opined it was an impossible case to defend and would I help try it. Oddly, the circumstance that the Marquette County Circuit Court would be the ultimate forum of a jury trial counted in controlling my response. I accepted. This was going to be new and exciting.

The preliminary examination was nondescript. The girl, aged 18, testified that one George Edwards, a truckdriver, oddly from my area in Southwestern Michigan, aged 32, had come uninvited to a beer bash at her parents' home while they were on a Wisconsin vacation. Edwards had stayed after all the 19 and 20 year olds had departed and it was charged he forced his way into her bedroom and raped her after striking her about the face. She had reported the assault to the Sheriff's office immediately after the man left. The magistrate had no trouble binding Edwards over for trial in Marquette County circuit Court. I wondered why I was in the case. It did not seem winnable..

The trial was an astonishing spectacle. A jury of seven women and five men — of the same complexion as the movie "Anatomy of a Murder" — was empaneled. Circuit Court Judge Donaldson, on the bench for many years, was an experienced and competent jurist. He was the sitting judge of the Court at the time of the movie setting, but his role had been played by Welch of McCarthy Committee fame. The prosecutor was a competent young lawyer who surely did not conceive he was going to have any trouble with the case. The bailiff seemed to be strangely familiar and I immediately recognized him when he called the Court to order as the bailiff who had played that particular role in the movie. The Courtroom, just as it appeared in the movie, was magnificent. The staircase and walls of the stairs to the Courtroom were marbled. The Courtroom itself was large, ample, marbled and elegant. I was shown the marble staircase which had reportedly been cracked by the load of heavy movie equipment that had been hauled up for the screening of "Anatomy of a Murder."

The prosecutor offered the Defendant a plea bargain. Namely, if he would plead guilty to attempted rape, rather than rape, he would confront a maximum of 15 years imprisonment instead of life. He refused though I recommended it.

I do not remember the name of my co-counsel whose case it originally was. He told me he had been a partner of Justice Volkers when the latter practiced law. I was tempted to ask him to invite Volkers to attend in order to secure follow-up script for a sequel movie. I had begun to revolve in my mind a program, "Anatomy of a Rape," which would be an apt second volume to the "Anatomy of a Murder."

The prosecution proofs followed faithfully those presented at the preliminary examination, except that there were introduced the youthful participants at the beer bash. They were surprised to see a man of Edwards age show up and no one knew him. The girl testified that after everyone had left, the Defendant had reappeared at the home, come into the bedroom and got into bed with her. When she had protested he slapped her about the face and threatened her. It was under such threat-that she had submitted. After he left she immediately reported the incident to the police. They were to confirm in Court and importantly to corroborate that there were marks of violence about her face.

When the prosecutor rested, my co-counsel told me he had more important business at the office and he was going to leave me alone. He felt that the case was a sure loser and he wanted to distance himself from it. There was some local angry attitude and deep resentment against Edwards. I had said I would try a case in Marquette County Circuit

Court and I was stuck with a highly improbable defense.

The Defendant George Edwards was a rake. He admitted his attraction to females and their easy response to him. He was a married man with a very lovely wife and two small children. Edwards was a philanderer and not one for whom much sympathy could be felt. His wife lived in Southern Michigan. She was a beautiful woman who had been a model for *Carson Pirie Scott* in Chicago. I called her and asked if she would testify for him. I related the details of the girl's testimony at the preliminary examination. She promised she would be present and available at the start of the defense proofs. I had my doubts she would show but at 8:30 a.m., the day our proofs were to start, I received a call from the desk of my hotel that she was there. She had flown in from Grand Rapids, Michigan, to Cadillac, Michigan, and then rented a car and had driven overland to Marquette. Despite her arduous trip, she looked as fresh as though she were a mannequin dressed in the most tasteful fashion for a show.

When I called her to the stand, members of the jury were attentive, upright and watched her every move and listened with rapt interest. She told us how long she had been married to Edwards. He was an incorrigible rake and philanderer, many times unfaithful. It seemed that he had a girl in every city he visited. He had a fatal attraction somehow for women and he had had many affairs. The man had one redeeming virtue: he would tell the truth even if it killed him! She was a magnificent witness and her testimony provided a credibility factor for George Edwards, otherwise impossible. I was to ask her if she was going to reconcile with him, for they were separated. She was adamantly to say no way. She had had enough of his cheating and would not go back to him.

During recess of the trial, to my amazement, I saw George in deep conversation with a tall good-looking brunette in the rear of the Courtroom. She came up to me and engaged me in some conversation. How did it happen she knew George Edwards? She was to tell me she was there only because she had heard of my Court trials and wanted to see me in action. I knew there was no truth to those remarks. Edwards was again plying his philander role, even in the courtroom.

I was ready to call Edwards to the stand. The jury had a new standard by which to judge his testimony. Here was an admitted rake, but his reputation for veracity had been vouchsafed by a long-suffering wife. The jury hung on his every word and they must have tested his statements by reference to his wife's testimony. He testified he was on a deer hunting trip and heard talk of a high school Beer Bash at some girl's home in the evening. He came uninvited, mingled and drank beer with the rest. When everyone had left, about 1:30 in the morning, he had returned and stood at the open door of the staircase leading to the second floor. He testified the girl, dressed in a diaphanous nightgown illuminating her figure, stood at the head of the stairs and beckoned him to come up. The two of them ultimately got in bed. At one point the girl protested. Angered that she was playing cat and mouse with him, he had slapped her. She had turned to him in pain, and said "You didn't have to do that," and he went on to say they had relations entirely with her full consent.

I do not totally remember the prosecutor's argument. He had some convincing proofs to sum up and he did very well. He argued the rape of the complainant. She had resisted the assault as demonstrated by the marks of slapping violence on her cheeks. She had quickly reported the assault, within 30 minutes of the occurrence. She would not have done this if she had voluntarily submitted to Edwards. The girl was the victim of a vicious rapist, and worse, the rapist had caused her to become pregnant. The die seemed cast. The Defendant was a reprehensible rake and should be so convicted.

I was alone to argue for the Defendant and then only once. I too condemned him as a rake and a philanderer who was unfaithful to his wife. He was worthy of absolutely no sympathy from the jury. Sympathy for the girl or antipathy for Edwards could not control the deliberations of the jury. I reminded them of the "Anatomy of a Murder" movie filmed in this very courtroom. This jury of seven women and five men were in fact arbiters of a sequel to that case. They were to critically examine and define the profile of the "Anatomy of a Rape." The Defendant was a wicked man. He had uninvitedly intruded on a teen party. What business did a 32 year old man have with such an affair? He was a cruel fellow, he had slapped the girl so hard about the face as to leave red marks on her cheeks, which the sheriff had verified. He had contributed to the girl's delinquency. He had caused her to become pregnant and certainly was subject to a paternity action.

The jury looked at me quizzically. I was talking like a prosecutor. I was bringing down a community-sensitive condemnation on the head of my client and I did it with conviction, for his conduct was revolting to me.

However, I pointed out that the facts in this case did not rise to a rape. The jury could not convict him for rape. If the prosecution had included the charge of contributing to the delinquency of a minor, there would be no question about a conviction quickly. This was no rape. The girl, though slapped, had protested that it was not necessary and she had consented to the relationship. The included charge of attempted rape, which the prosecutor had at minimum urged as an included offense, was a cop-out. If it was not rape, it could not be an attempted rape. It clearly was an assault and battery. I told the jury to critically examine the proofs and have no sympathy with the Defendant and hold him strictly accountable for what he had done, namely, the beating of the girl, and not for an offense such as rape or attempted rape for which he was no more guilty than murder. They might suspect his guilt, but suspicion was not enough. They had to be convinced of his guilt of rape beyond a reasonable doubt. His wife's candid assessment of him as a "no good wife-cheating scalawag" who had a woman in every port, but who had the redeeming virtue of "telling the truth even if it killed him," placed in full focus this man's involvement. He was an aggressive hunter of women who found him irresistible. I should have liked to have applied a law to castrate him but there was no such law and the jury could supply none. I was finally to urge that they limit themselves to the definition of the profile of an

"Anatomy of a Rape" and, if they agreed with me, they find the Defendant not guilty of rape or attempted rape. However, I insisted they find him guilty of assault and battery of the complaining witness.

My wife Rachel, characteristically, and my son Jack, who had recently graduated from law school, with his new wife, Julie, were in the audience. They gave me no comfort after my summation. If Rachel or Julie had been on the jury the result may very well have been different. This jury returned a verdict of not guilty of rape and not guilty of attempted rape, but guilty of assault and battery.

What transpired thereafter, to say the least, was bizarre. The presiding judge took me and the prosecutor into his chambers. "You know," he said to me, "you have secured an astounding result. I would have found him guilty of rape very quickly. I shall give him the maximum of 90 days in the local jail for the assault and battery conviction." I could not quarrel with the sentence assessment and I reported the same to the Defendant before he was presented to the Court.

To my surprise and chagrin, he was to complain bitterly. He was a cross-country trucker who owned a big 18-wheel truck which he drove carrying merchandise and loads all the way between the two coasts. The rig was a new one valued at at least $30,000 and was heavily liened. If he were denied its use for that span of time, the equipment would be repossessed and he would lose his entire equity. It seemed to him grossly unfair.

My explanation that the sentence was the judge's prerogative was unavailing. Despairing of satisfying him, I addressed the Court with the Defendant at my side and I related his plight. The Court, to my surprise, was considerate. He would assess 30 days, not the maximum of 90. The client tucked at my sleeve and called me aside, with permission granted by the Court. He whispered that 30 days was just as bad as 90 days. The equipment idled would be repossessed and he would be ruined. Shaken, I turned back to the Court and protested that the 30 day incarceration would just as surely spell financial ruin for him, not just punishment. The Court mused something about 30 days done on consecutive weekends. Again the client tugged at my sleeves and whispered that if he was at the end of his trip on a weekend in San Francisco, how in the world would he be able to make it back to Marquette, Michigan?

I suggested a chambers discussion with the Court. I had no desire to continue the haggling over the sentence. In chambers, an exasperated Judge confronted me and shortly told me he wanted both my client and me as quickly as possible out of Marquette County. He would deputize me to take custody of my client and deposit him with the Berrien County Sheriff's Office which happenstance was his county of residence, for service there in the county a term of 30 days spent on consecutive weekends.

The Defendant was understandably elated. I was in truth eager to be rid of him. He had the audacity to say to my wife with all the syrupy nuances of a man on the loose, "You know, Mrs. Keller, I am now going to be in your custody for a while." Rachel is a very beautiful woman and we have always been devoted to each other. She was repulsed by his advance. I was totally relieved to be finally discharged of my custody of him by turning him over to the Berrien County Sheriff's Office. I should like to believe that he was faithful in serving out his weekend terms.

When Justice Volkers completed his successful defense of the Army Lieutenant charged with murder of the philandering bartender who had made indecent approaches to his wife, he was never paid a fee. The Lieutenant's last words to him were "See you later, Buster." Volkers was angry. He took out his anger by writing a bestseller, "Anatomy of a Murder" and sold the movie rights. His fee, if paid, would have been insignificant compared to his draw on the sale of the book and the movie rights. I was paid a small fee, but I never wrote the sequel "Anatomy of a Rape." Possibly I should have.

PEOPLE VS. D'ANGELO — A STING OPERATION THAT BACKFIRED AND WENT TO THE SUPREME COURT

In the climate of 1984-85, I had followed the DeLorean criminal prosecution with mixed feelings. The Federal Government had mounted and relied on an elaborate sting operation to nail DeLorean. Federal procedure had allowed the entire issue to be determined by a jury, and the jury had returned a verdict of not guilty to the surprise of many.

I had participated in an appeal in 1976 to the Supreme Court of Michigan, which significantly had contributed to a change in the Michigan criminal legal procedure affecting the prosecution of narcotic cases, where the defense of entrapment was asserted.

The facts surrounding the case were challenging. Dominic D'Angelo had been convicted after a two-day jury trial before Berrien Circuit Judge Julian Hughes in 1977, of the offense of Sale and Delivery of LSD, a controlled substance, which carried a possible twenty-year sentence. Our defense had been entrapment, namely that the police had stooped to a sting operation, whereby they had created, indeed manufactured, a criminal offense, by entrapping the defendant into a criminal transaction which he would not have entertained but for their intervention. We could get no hearing before the trial judge prior to submission to the jury, and my motion for a directed verdict at the close of the proofs on the ground that entrapment had been established by uncontroverted evidence, was denied. Entrapment, along with other fact issues, was submitted to the jury, a panel which characteristically regarding the defendant alone to be on trial, shortly returned a verdict of guilty.

In the case of People v. Turner, 390 Mich Report, page 7 (1973), a non-jury case, a majority of the Michigan Supreme Court had determined that thenceforth the objective test of the entrapment defense, focusing only on police conduct or misconduct, not the predisposition of the defendant, was to be employed by the Trial Court to determine whether entrapment by the police instigating the criminal act had been proven. However, the precise question whether in a jury trial, the judge or the jury should determine and resolve the entrapment defense was not confronted. Throughout the state, jurists were in a quandary as to how to handle the issue of entrapment when raised as a defense in a jury case. And it was being raised many times in drug cases throughout Michigan. The Turner decision, borrowing heavily from the minority opinions of U.S. Supreme Court Justices Stewart, Roberts, Brandeis and Frankfurter, clearly turned the Michigan criminal jurisprudence away from the subjective test which had permitted the jury as trier of the facts to consider both the police activity and the predisposition, past record and activity of the defendant, together with his predisposition to commit the offense and return a general verdict. A general verdict of guilty characteristically focuses only on the defendant. Under the subjective test, reprehensible police activity, creating and producing crime, asserted by the defense of entrapment, is likely to be relegated to secondary priority, regardless how destructive of due process concern for police policy entrapment procedure is.

There understandably was much criticism in legal circles of the subjective test, and the Turner decision was conceived to be the approach best calculated as a matter of public policy to condemn and discourage impermissible police conduct which had the effect of manufacturing crime.

In the D'Angelo case, the reprehensible effect of a police sting operation manufacturing crime out of the thin air, and the proclivity of a general jury verdict to focus on naught but the defendant on trial was starkly demonstrated. D'Angelo and his friends were gathered in one of the parties' apartment. Admittedly, some of them were smoking marijuana. One Clifford Murphy, a hired informant of the Berrien County Metro Unit, showed up at approximately 10 p.m. of February 2, 1975, and was with the group only a short time. D'Angelo and his friends related that Murphy had tried without success to sell to those present some green tablets which he called Mescaline. He finally approached the defendant for a loan of $5, claiming he needed it to go out on a date, received the sum of $5 from the defendant D'Angelo and gave him three tablets as security for repayment. He promised to repay the loan the next day. D'Angelo testified that in fact the next day Murphy had appeared at his apartment, repaid the $5 loan, and he had given him back the three tablets of Mescaline. The prosecution was to introduce as an exhibit at the trial of the case the three tablets, asserting there was a sale of drugs accomplished. Murphy, wired by the police, had knocked on the defendant's apartment's door and said to D'Angelo: "Here's you $5. Where's my stuff?" The police were waiting, and Murphy turned over to them the tape and three tablets which the prosecution entered as evidentiary exhibit. They were to argue that this constituted irrefutable proof that Murphy had purchased the three tablets of controlled substance from the defendant.

Murphy, on cross examination, was evasive, but he admitted that he may have been in the apartment a short time the evening of February 2, 1975. He was to claim he didn't remember anything of the evening's affair, but he couldn't deny the three tablets of Mescaline which he had secured from D'Angelo were actually in his possession on February 2. Significantly he did not deny that he had tried unsuccessfully to sell them to the people in the apartment. Importantly when pressed, he was unable to deny that he told D'Angelo he wanted a loan of $5 and would give him the three tablets as security. Finally, he could not deny the three tablets he had taken back from D'Angelo the next day on February 3 when the loan of $5 was repaid were the same tablets which had been in his possession the prior evening and which he had turned over to D'Angelo as security.

On the basis of this testimony, the case against the defendant came down to a collusive, contrived and deliberate effort on the part of Murphy, acting under the control and direction of local Metro police officers, to induce the defendant to commit a criminal offense for which he could be later prosecuted. My motion for a directed verdict was denied, and the jury obviously not focusing objectively on reprehensible police activity which had stooped to use this kind of murky, hired testimony, returned a verdict of guilty. To the trial judge's credit, my motion before sentence to set aside the conviction and quash the proceedings or grant at least a new trial on the ground that the Court had erred on submitting the issue of entrapment to the jury, was granted. The prosecutor was ordered to take forthwith an appeal to the Supreme Court bypassing the Court of Appeals.

The three sitting Berrien judges, Chester Byrns, Julian Hughes and William S. White, alluding to the entrapment defense often raised in narcotics cases, joined in an unusual certification to the Supreme Court asking that Court to forthwith address the procedural manner of handling the defense, for the law was indeed confused and uncertain. Turner had indeed adopted the objective test in entrapment focusing on the propriety of government conduct, instead of the defendant's supposed "predisposition to commit a crime." However, Turner had been a judge trial and no jury was involved.

The Supreme Court's decision after argument was a resounding affirmance of the requirement for determination of the defense of entrapment by the Court only. * Justice Ryan writing a majority opinion affirmed the Trial Court's order of a new trial and directed that the issue of entrapment be determined by the Court and the case be dismissed and the defendant discharged if the trial judge concluded that the defendant indeed had been entrapped by impermissible conduct of the police. The charges against D'Angelo were subsequently dismissed after such a finding by the Court that he was entrapped.

*People vs. D'Angelo, 401 Mich 167, 257 NW2d655.

Of key importance to Michigan jurisprudence was the following in Justice Ryan's majority opinion:

"The policy considerations which moved us to adopt the objective test of entrapment compel with equal force the conclusion that the judge and not the jury must determine its existence. The thesis is that law enforcement conduct which essentially manufactures crime is a corruptive use of governmental authority which, when used to obtain a conviction, taints the judiciary which tolerates its use. It is a practice which relies for success upon judicial indifference, if not approval, and it must be deterred. Its deterrence is a duty which transcends the determination of guilt or innocence in a given case and it stands ultimately as the responsibility of an incorruptible judiciary."

Henceforth throughout Michigan, Trial Courts were mandated when the defendant raised the entrapment defense to conduct an evidentiary hearing, in the jury's absence, wherein the previous disposition of any defendant to commit an offense would be irrelevant and the focus would objectively be on the questioned police activity.

Justice Mennen Williams, who was in my entering University of Michigan law class of 1936, wrote a lone dissent, complaining that the police were being unduly shackled in the tactics they could employ in cases involving difficult detection. He had dissented in the case of People vs.Turner taking the position that the subjective test involving the predisposition of the defendant to commit a crime was relevant and could be considered by a jury, and his dissent therefore in the D'Angelo case was consistent.

I had the satisfaction of feeling I had left some small mark on the State's criminal jurisprudence.

GENERAL MOTORS' MOTOR MOUNT CASE GETS TO THE JURY

On July 8, 1972, Elva Nelson, a woman in her mid 70's, was driving her 1965 Chevrolet Station Wagon on Red Arrow Highway near Harbert, Michigan, with six of her friends enroute to a bridge game at her home in Sawyer, Michigan. She had stopped off the highway and walked across it to a bakery to buy some pastry for the party. Back in her car and starting up from a stop, she accelerated up a slight rise in the highway and, following the curve in the road, had turned her wheels to the left. The automobile suddenly accelerating on the curve, went out of control. She screamed and the car slammed into a tree off the highway. Two of her passengers were killed and four were injured.

When Mrs. Nelson died some two years later of a cause unrelated to the accident, two of the surviving passengers, Florence Mathews and Dorothy Iddel, retained Henry Gleiss to represent them in a cause of action for negligence against the Estate of Elva Nelson, the driver. Mrs. Nelson had three passengers in the front seat. These four occupants were one too many to permit a careful operation of the automobile. It appeared the injured passengers did have a viable cause of action against the driver for not leaving herself enough room in the front seat to adequately and properly maneuver her automobile.

A law firm in Chicago referred to me the cases of the two other surviving passengers, Winifred Dorscheid, aged 84 years, and Dorothy Loskill, aged 78 years, expecting that I would join in the action against the Estate of the deceased driver asserting her negligence for the injuries to these passengers.

Upon my investigation of the action, it appeared to me that the better action was against General Motors for the negligent manufacture of the automobile. I convinced Attorney Gleiss to join with me in such an action rather than to proceed wholly against the Nelson Estate.

In May, 1972, General Motors had sent out to approximately seven million purchasers of its Chevrolet automobiles, model years 1965 through 1971, a recall notice advising them of a possible hazard in such automobiles, involving a defective motor mount. Under certain conditions, such as acceleration from a stop or slow speed, going around a curve, the motor mount could lift off and separate. This could cause the accelerator harness to hang up and stick, resulting in sudden acceleration of the automobile.

Mrs. Nelson's 1965 Chevrolet Station Wagon had been purchased new in 1965. As far as she knew she had not had any difficulty with it. When she received the recall letter she had taken it to the Don Leitow Chevrolet Dealership in Bridgman, Michigan, to have the suggested corrective part installed. That dealership had not received the part and the accident occurred a few months later.

There had been no motor mount case successfully prosecuted against General Motors to a jury verdict in Michigan, and this was a route I wished to take. After the case was filed I plied General Motors with Interrogatories and it was to admit that from 1966 through 1971, it had received over 2,000 complaints from Chevrolet owners and replaced over 100,000 motor mounts in the period 1965 through 1969 on

Chevrolets of the questioned model years, all before May of 1972. Importantly, General Motors was to admit it knew about the defects as early as 1966, but took no action to advise owners of the cars with the defective part until 1972. It had first offered to correct the faulty motor mount in 1972 when it sent out the recall letter in May of that year. Here was a classic case of manufacturer's neglect. Circuit Court Judge Zoe S. Burkholz had no difficulty in overruling the defense motion to dismiss the case.

Attorneys about the country were bringing on these cases. Attorney William Reamon of Grand Rapids had headed up a Motor Mount Clearinghouse, to which I initially subscribed. There was a great deal of legwork and preparation to do, but it was an incomparably better and more rewarding negligence action against the "big pocket" of General Motors, than the limited insurance coverage of the deceased driver, Elva Nelson.

I retained as consultant noted automotive engineer, Jay Bold, Professor of Automotive Engineering at the University of Michigan. His deposition was taken. He knew of the problem, the complaints of motorists, and the recall letter, and he articulated the mechanism of the failure which would cause the accelerator to hang up. General Motors had taken the position that any intelligent motorist would have shut off the ignition and the motor would have stalled. The suggestion was clear. The driver Elva Nelson, in her middle 70's, knew of the problem and the danger and she exposed her friends wittingly to it. Indeed she had exacerbated the situation by crowding four occupants into the front seat. She had culpably failed to turn off the ignition and control the automobile. The corporate argument was rudimentary and shallow. A 75 year old widow confronted with a suddenly accelerating car, speeding at full throttle and out of control could be reasonably expected to panic and not know what to do!

We determined not to call Professor Bolt live to the stand. He had a graduate student drive a 1965 Chevrolet with a broken motor mount to duplicate the accelerator hang up, but this had been less than successful.

I had scoured the area for a 'grease monkey' mechanic who had worked on the repair of Chevrolets of the recall vintage and knew of the motor mount problem. I wanted someone to come into Court with work grease on his pants. I found such a mechanic who not only had worked on the Chevrolet series 1965 to 1971 and repaired motor mounts, but who personally knew of the problem the result of a failure causing sudden acceleration in his own Chevrolet model automobile year 1967. That car had suddenly accelerated from a slow speed going up an inclining curve in St. Joseph, Michigan, to full throttle. He knew immediately what had happened and turned off the ignition, thereby averting tragedy. He was a vigorous young man of 29 years and his reaction time was quick. When checking his car in the garage, the mechanic identified, as he suspected, the defective broken motor mount, and made his own repair and correction of the mount. His telling of his experience, background training and acquaintance with the problem was dramatic. The defense was not able to blunt his testimony which was to have many times the value of even the most distinguished engineering professor.

Here was someone who was acquainted with the problem, had lived through a terrifying confrontation with it, and had coped with the emergency so he could stop the automobile without endangering his life.

The General Motors defense was to put on screen a videocassette of a testdriver who put a 1965 Chevrolet with faulty motor mount through a course of travel designed to lift the mount and cause an accelerator harness hang up, all without incident. It was interesting and instructive, but it did not detract from the grease mechanic's testimony.

The jury was out four hours to end a nine day trial. During argument, one of my clients, Winifred Dorscheid, aged 84, the oldest of the Plaintiffs, fell asleep and indeed snored. The average age of the four Plaintiffs was 77 years. The jury must have fallen in love with these elderly women who had been injured through no fault on their part. The defense was correct, their life expectancy was limited, but General Motor's negligence was clear cut.

The jury returned a verdict of $67,314 for my client, Dorothy Loskill, aged 78 years, and $28,865 for my client, Winifred Dorscheid, aged 84 years. A total verdict in favor of all Plaintiffs in the amount of $162,637 was returned by the jury. The General Motors attorney said there would be an appeal. I hoped there would be because no motor mount case had been reported on appeal. I was disappointed when the full award plus interest from date of filing was paid. General Motors did not want the verdict reported on appeal. It was eminently a more satisfying lawsuit than one limited to the deceased driver, Elva Nelson, who was herself a victim of manufacturer's negligence.

GROENING VS. NOWLEN'S PLYWOOD INN: THE CASE OF THE BOOKKEEPER WHO CLAIMED HE HAD ONLY TAKEN $400

Otto Groening, a widower in his late 60's, had for a number of years from 1953 to June 24, 1960, been bookkeeper for Bud Nowlen's Plywood Inn in St. Joseph. On that last date, his employer caused him to be arrested and taken into custody of the St. Joseph Police Station on the charge that he had embezzled a large sum of money from the Plywood Inn. Nowlen retained John Globensky to represent him, and the bookkeeper, already in custody and jailed, was threatened with criminal prosecution unless he executed and delivered to his employer a warranty deed, conveying his residence. This he did ultimately by signing a deed dated June 25, 1960, attesting it his "free and voluntary act" in the presence of Attorney Globensky who acted as notary public and Pastor Franz Victorsen, Otto's minister. Nowlen was to claim that the warranty deed was executed freely and voluntarily by the bookkeeper for the sole purpose of making restitution of monies which he had taken from the Nowlen firm during the years 1958, '59 and '60, approximating $25,000 to $35,000. Nowlen and his attorney also claimed the Groening real estate would be held in trust until the amount of the embezzlement could be ascertained by an accounting whereupon the property would be sold and proceeds used only to restore the embezzled monies. Indeed, Nowlen in turn signed a quit-claim deed dated June 25, 1960, to be held in trust pending such accounting.

Groening was promptly released a free man on the Friday evening he signed the deed. He sought me out early the Monday following. He admitted he had converted $400 over a period of time but protested that was the extent of any conversion and he had given Nowlen a personal check for such sum in the police station. He vigorously denied any conversion or embezzlement in excess of $400. I could understand the desire of the employer to secure restitution of a feared much greater embezzlement. I was revolted, however, at the maneuver to arrest and imprison a man and then threaten him with a criminal prosecution unless he forfeit his home. This smacked of a power over the prosecutor of a criminal charge which no private citizen should assert. The employer and his attorney had secured the arrest and literal jailing of the man and then threatened him with a criminal prosecution and ultimate imprisonment unless he sign over his home. This certainly was no free and voluntary act on his part. He signed the deed before a notary public under duress and compulsion of such threats.

Groening related to me that his employer supervised and shared the charge, control and management of the business of bookkeeping operations. He admitted he had wrongfully taken $400, but insisted he was being victimized and charged falsely with huge inventory shrinkage, bad business management and imprudent ventures of his employer, over which he had no control or responsibility. The $400, taken in small sums regularly with the intent to pay them back, left him in a peculiarly vulnerable position. Why had the employer taken from him a check for $400, the amount of his confessed conversion?

My review of the facts given me that Monday by Groening concluded in the prompt filing of a complaint in Berrien Circuit Court on June 24, 1960. It asserted that Nowlen had threatened Groening with criminal prosecution for embezzlement unless the latter executed and delivered a warranty deed to his home. Groening, under fear and duress, did so. The consideration — compounding a felony — was illegal and no notary public should have under oath verified a free and voluntary act.

John Globensky, an astute, able and successful tax and corporation attorney, surely must early have had misgivings about his notarization of the deed. He had known and served Bud Nowlen for years and certainly must have believed Groening had embezzled from his client large sums approximating $25,000 to $35,000, far more than the $400 which Groening admitted. He was concerned, as well he should have been, with protecting his client and securing restitution. I have no doubt Globensky had some affection for the bookkeeper whom he had known for some years. He certainly didn't relish the idea of prosecution and imprisonment of the old man. It must have seemed to him a clean and proper way to handle a messy matter to the benefit of a good client with the cooperation of the police and the prosecutor's office, which had authorized the warrant. Globensky also had the foresight to call in the bookkeeper's pastor, Franz Victorsen, pastor of the Saron Lutheran Church in St. Joseph, to act as witness along with him to the deed of conveyance. A man of God would witness the conveyance along with a notary public! This was calculated to confer the maximum validity to the instrument. The inclusion of the minister as a witness to the deed was to profoundly affect the trial in a way Attorney Globensky could not have foreseen.

John called in to his firm Henry Gleiss to handle the case. Many fine lawyers eschew trial litigation and prefer the office practice of tax, corporate, probate work and consultations. It was always my impression that Globensky preferred the office practice. In any event, he couldn't handle this defense for he had the conflict of his personal involvement. Gleiss was establishing himself in an association with the late Robert Feldman, a worker's compensation attorney, as having a yen for the trial pit, and it was to him that Globensky entrusted the defense of the case which was destined to go to the Supreme Court.

At trial, Groening testified that in the police station he admitted taking small sums from the Nowlen concern, but when he was charged with taking $25,000 to $35,000, he vigorously protested this was not so. With Nowlen and his attorney present, interrogation continued for over five hours with different officers participating. Groening testified he had said to them: "What can I do? I can tell you from now to Christmas that I don't know anything more. I have no connection with $25,000. Right now you appear to me as monsters, and I sit here in this chair like a little mouse. What can I do?" The experience physically and mentally sickened him. He felt dirty. He said one of the officers said to him: "We don't want to get tough with you, but we can. You can get five to ten years at Jackson Penitentiary if you don't make a clean breast of it, and with your heart condition you wouldn't last a month. They would throw you into a meat wagon." Groening had turned to his employer for help, and the latter said it was out of his hands. Desperate and having no friends, he testified: "When I found I could not get together with Mr. Nowlen, the thought occurred to me that everything was against me so when I was asked if I would sign my home over to Mr. Nowlen, I said I would because I had no chance in the police station to clear myself and make these men believe me."

After five hours of such questioning, around 10 p.m. he first saw his minister come in with Attorney Globensky and the police chief.

The minister had a few words with Groening before the deed was signed and witnessed. The pastor said to him: "Otto, you must make restitution for what you have taken." Groening had replied: "Sure, but you see, Pastor, I have no friends here." The minister had assured him he was a friend. Groening testified he never had opportunity to be alone with his minister <u>before</u> he signed the deed.

After signing the instrument, he had asked for a conference alone with the Pastor and there, to be confirmed by the pastor's testimony later, a strange interlude occurred. Victorsen told Otto he has sinned against God and man and must come to church to confess and take communion. Groening had told him he had nothing to confess other than a small amount of conversion he had admitted. The minister had turned to go and tell the others but Groening had held him back, put his fingers to his lips and begged the minister to say nothing and be quiet for the room was tapped and he was afraid. He had to get out of this jail to clear himself!

Pastor Victorsen testified that he had been brought by police patrol from an outdoor theater to the police station shortly before 9 p.m. and at once taken to the chief's office. Nowlen, Attorney Globensky, and a legal secretary were there. Groening was not there, and for about an hour the minister was filled in the details of an alleged $25,000 to $35,000 embezzlement by the bookkeeper. He was given the impression they had caught him with the evidence, that he had confessed and they were being lenient with him because of a heart condition.

Victorsen testified "they thought if he was sent to jail he would die in a month. I felt they were being very charitable and kind to him since he had confessed to embezzlement of this sum of money." Only after this hour session at which Groening was not present did Victorsen see his parishioner who was brought into the room. Otto looked distraught and was not in his usual command of self. He was unkempt and the pastor noted that instead of his normal immaculately groomed appearance, his white hair looked dull as though he had been running his hands through it. He was nervous and flushed. The deed was brought in and Pastor Victorsen and Globensky signed it as witnesses after Groening had signed it. Up to that time the minister had had no opportunity to talk or be alone with Groening. The minister, then, was asked if he wished to be alone with him and when he assented, the others left the room. Pastor Victorsen then turned to Groening and inquired why he had embezzled the money. The following testimony was given by the minister on direct examination by me in Court (Joint Appendus in Supreme Court Pages 51a, 52a and 53a):

Q: What did he say to you?

A: That's when he told me he didn't do it.

Q: What did he say?

A: I was about to turn and go out the door, thinking I should tell the others about this.

Q: What did he say, as best you can recall it?

A: Well, I had told him that he would have to come to church the next morning. I wanted him to come down there to confess his sins, then in order that he might be able to receive communion. This is a regular procedure in discipline in the church for a man who has sinned grievously before God and man. Before he can be restored to Holy Communion, he must come to his pastor and tell him the whole story, and then he can receive Holy Communion, and then I mentioned the word "confessed," and he said, "Pastor, I don't have anything to confess." It was then that he informed me that he didn't take twenty-five or thirty-five thousand dollars, and it was at that point that I was about to go out of the room, and he called me back.

Q: And what did he say?

A: I said, "We will have to tell the others," or "We should tell the others." He said, "No, I have got to get out of here." He said, "I can't defend myself in this jail."

Q: Did he speak in a normal voice, a loud voice, or a soft voice, or did he whisper?

A: He spoke in a very soft whisper, and cautioned me to speak softly, because, he said, "I think this room has been tapped."

Q: And when he cautioned you in that manner, did he put his finger to his lips?

A: Yes.

Q: Was there any other conversation between you at that time, that you recall?

A: I tried to find out a little more about the situation, but all that he could say was that "I'm not guilty. I haven't taken $35,000. I did take $400. I am going to make restitution for that." And that was about the extent of our conversation.

Q: What happened next?

A: The group came back from the outer office then, with the agreement that was to be signed.

****

Q: All right, what happened next?

A: We signed the agreement, and shortly thereafter I took my leave of the group, and Mr. Groening, and went on my way. They sent me back to the theatre in a patrol car.

****

Q: Did you have any further discussion after the others came into the room? After your previous conference with Mr. Groening before, did you have any further discussion with him before he signed this agreement, exhibit 3?

A: No, I did not.

Q: How long after the others came in was it that he signed this agreement?

A: Almost immediately.

****

Q: And did you tell at that time Mr. Globensky or Chief Gillespie or anyone else of the conversation you had alone with Mr. Groening?

A: I did not.

Q: Why didn't you?

A: Because it was a pastoral conference.

Q: It was a confidential relationship?

A: It was.

Q: And he had admonished you not to tell anyone?

A: That's correct.

Q: Does this impress a duty upon you to not reveal it?

A: By all means. It's a vow of ordination.

The testimony of the officers, the prosecuting attorney, who authorized warrant for larceny from a building and then dismissed it, and finally the testimony of John Globensky were anticlimax. John confirmed that either on June 27 or June 28, 1960, the following week, he had a discussion with Pastor Victorsen with only minor deviation from the testimony in Court.

The minister had in detail related to him the same sequence of events he testified to in open Court. Globensky had also told the minister in that conversation that indeed the Chief's office was bugged with a squawk box," but that when Groening talked alone with him, nobody heard the conversation. Groening therefore had good reason to fear the room he was in with anyone was tapped. Globensky was always convinced there were only three things wanted by Groening, namely, (1) he wanted to make restitution, (2) he wanted the matter to be quieted down, and (3) he did not want to go to jail!

The defense could not possibly win. I moved for an instructed verdict on the grounds of duress and undue influence. Trial Judge Hadsell found that Groening had indeed executed the deed and contract on the implied promise he would not be criminally prosecuted and therefore the instruments were void as against public policy. The premises were to be redeeded to him. The Judge however would not go so far as to taint the defense with duress and undue influence. Additionally, he assigned to a Circuit Court commissioner the matter of determination, what if any amount Groening owed Nowlen following an accounting. I do not recall that any further determination was made on that matter.

Nowlen's counsel took appeal to the Supreme Court and that forum affirmed the Trial Judge, <u>Groening vs. Nowlen Plywood Inn</u>, 369 Mich 28.

RELATIONSHIP BETWEEN LAWYERS

A well-understood and hopefully maintained attitude of trial practitioners to each other is that, while one may and should vigorously and with full devotion advance a client's cause against the adversary, after the case is concluded, opposing attorneys typically maintain friendly relations with each other. Clients who involve themselves in emotionally draining contests with others, formerly regarded as friends, most often leave such disputes permanently estranged from their opposite numbers. In the trial forum it is the duty of each attorney to vigorously advance his client's cause. Any other approach would be a betrayal of the trust placed in him. A basic civility between contesting trial lawyers, however, requires that they maintain continuing respect for each other in and out of the courtroom. Trial practice would be an intolerably cruel area if this were not so.

There was only one attorney for whom I could not maintain this approach. Joseph Killian and I were implacable foes in and out of the courtroom for over twenty-five years. During that period, neither of us spoke to each other except in the stress of court conflict. It all started in a divorce action and before I had pledged to abstain from domestic litigation. It is possible that my differences with Killian had some influence on my leaving that field.

Dr. Charles Ozeran was a good family practitioner in Benton Harbor during the '40's and '50's. He was one of the few doctors who into the '60's made house calls. I had known him for many years, going back to my University of Michigan days when I had waited table and served him and his first wife, Edith, as students there. I had represented his first wife when he divorced her. When his second wife brought her action against him, Killian represented the doctor, and I represented the second wife. The doctor was a very generous and open-minded man and had promised his wife a certain property as part of her settlement, in apparent opposition to Killian's advice. When she was cross-examined about property matters by Killian, she came out suddenly with the bald statement that her husband wanted her to have this property, and the doctor in open court agreed to it. I was as surprised as Joe, but not at all as upset. Killian was furious and accused me of being party to an arrangement behind his back As vigorously, I denied any such purpose on my part. Joe then gave forth with a slurring epithet, impugning my religion, which slur I regarded as repugnant and contemptible. I answered him with some anger, suggesting an epithet casting in doubt his legitimacy and told him that I should not again speak civilly to him and expected his like attitude. It was the beginning of a twenty-five year feud which knew no counterpart in Berrien county legal history.

Joe Killian was a hard-driven and competent lawyer. He had been an assistant prosecutor under Tony Westin until the latter was elevated to the bench. As prosecutor, he wielded a great deal of power in the county. His assistant prosecutors went on to become judges, and it was said of him that he carried enough influence to determine the destiny of any candidate for public office. I had occasion to try many cases with him, and they were all hard fought, no quarter given. He was ultimately to limit his practice to condemnation suits, and our court contests, except one shortly to be related, ended. Joe was a man you either loved or hated. His friends were legion and so were those who disliked him, in which latter category I was numbered. His courage and devotion to friends was legendary. One incident stood out: He had taken out in his boat several friends in the '50's. A storm had tossed the boat over some five miles from shore. It was said of him and I believe it, that Joe marshaled the courage and discipline of everyone by his own example, to cling to the boat and was personally responsible for their ultimate safety.

An accident occurred May 21, 1960, which was to test my attitude towards Joe Killian. Oliver Slater, a patrolman for the Benton Harbor Police Department, had suffered permanent injuries in a three-car collision, which caused him to be hospitalized over three months. Slater and another officer had chased two boys riding a motorcycle, taken them into custody and they were returning in their patrol car on Territorial Road in Benton Township when the seventeen-year-old son of Joe Killian, driving his mother's automobile, drove through a service station drive to cut in front of another car, lost control and collided head on with the patrol car. Slater asked my help. If there had been another local attorney involved, I would have eschewed the case. I brought suit for Slater against the boy and the mother who was the owner of the car, asking $180,000 damages. Killian retained Ted Hammond, an eminent trial attorney in Benton Harbor and the Seymour brothers (Dale and Dalton) to defend. The Circuit Judge disqualified himself and Wayne Circuit Judge Montante presided. The Michigan Auto Club carried Killian's insurance and never made any effort to settle the case, though the liability appeared unquestionable, until the Friday before trial began on Monday. Then for the first time, they summarily offered $60,000, probably at the time considered a fair offer. I refused to consider it, taking the position that trial was imminent.

The second day of trial in Judge Montante's chambers, defense attorneys commented I had refused a $60,000 offer. The judge raised his eyebrows, and I said I had no comment and was surprised the matter was even broached by defense counsel. I was prepared for trial. Outside the chambers, I was literally set upon by newspaper reporters. It was rumored I had refused a very large settlement offer and continued to demand the full $180,000 set forth in the declaration.

The circumstance that the editor of the local newspaper was a former assistant prosecutor under Joe Killian didn't assuage my suspicion that I was being set up. I made no comment to all inquiries other than to say that I was prepared to try the case.

The next issue of the local newspaper carried a very damaging news item on the first page. It stated therein that it was widely rumored about the courthouse I had refused a settlement of $60,000 and had insisted on the full $180,000 to the damage claim. To say the least, it was an unusual story. I had had no part in leaking any such story, and I was being victimized by it.

I didn't have long to wait developments. At the next morning's session of court after the news release, defense counsel Ted Hammond showed up with a newspaper under his arm. He had a motion to make out of the hearing of the jury. The motion was for a mistrial, because of the news item. I protested angrily that I had been set up. Indeed, the defense had not been prejudiced by the article even if it had come to the jurors' attention. I had been put in a bad light, and the Plaintiff, not the Defendants, had right to complain. But we were not complaining and wished the trial to go on. Judge Montante called in the jury. Two members had read the article. The Court ruled a mistrial.

My client, Ollie Slater, was devastated. His reaction mirrored mine, but he must have secured small solace from my assurance we would prevail. He was to continue to brood.

That summer I attended the American Trial Lawyers' convention in Boston. At the banquet meeting in the Ritz Hotel, I was called to the phone. It was defense attorney Dalton Seymour. He was embarrassed to tell me my client was in his office and wanted to settle, regardless of advice. It is an understatement to say this was an upsetting and unheard of turn of events. I told Dalton to tell my client to wait until I returned and to send him forth from his office. Upon my return, I found Slater disconsolate. He would not listen to any advice which I urged upon him to await a new trial. The case was ultimately settled at his demand for

$67,500, a sum I thought inadequate compensation for his very serious injuries.

Joe Killian and I did make up in a way. He had a serious liver problem and had sickened, lost weight and become very ill. I saw him at Tosi's Restaurant in south St. Joseph shortly before his death. Twenty-five years had passed without a civil word between us. Something impelled me — (the better angels of my nature?) — to go up to him. I stood by his chair, laid my hand on his shoulder and said, "Joe, I hope you make it." Joe looked up at me, placed his hand over mine and responded, "George, I am sure going to try." I was always glad we had made up, though belated by a long period of hostility, probably reflecting two strongly willed, stubborn antagonists who ought to have limited their opposition to each other to the court forum, but had not had the sense of personal discipline to do so.

THE IMPROVEMENT OF THE DOWNTOWN ST. JOSEPH AREA

An opportunity came in the late '70's to be of some service to the City of St. Joseph, Michigan, and that experience was as satisfying as any I had in court. Rachel, my wife, had been instrumental in the mid '70's in getting the City Commission stimulated to install artificial flowers on the light poles in the downtown area. It was an early attempt to bring a fresh ambiance to the downtown area and presaged later developments.

We owned real estate downtown and it was natural for her to seek to beautify the property. There were rumors of a big indoor mall coming to Benton Township and it was uneasily speculated that such a development could herald the demise of St. Joseph in the same manner the Fairplain Plaza had triggered the collapse and ultimate decay of the neighboring City of Benton Harbor.

"Project Foresight" was mounted to somehow prepare St. Joseph to entertain and implement a downtown revitalization and avoid Benton

Harbor's fate. Ultimately the City Commission created a Downtown Development Authority (DDA) under a legislative enactment and I was made the first Chairman. This was a position of responsibility largely earned through Rachel's labors to bring beauty, ambiance and vitality to the downtown section, which already showed signs of depression and deterioration.

The early DDA had distinguished personnel on it. Jack Sparks, the vice-president of Whirlpool, later to become the Chairman of the Board, served for several years as a Director. Bud Barlow, a local drycleaner, Ray Carlson, owner and manager of Ollie's, the largest department store in the downtown area, Les Hornack, investor, Mayor Frank Smith, Richard Schanze of People's State Bank, Ted Bestervelt of Troost Furniture, Clif Emlong, John Felters and others served as Directors. Ron Momany brought to his post of Executive Director enthusiasm and continuing guidance. William Sinclair, newly appointed City Manager, joined in energetically advancing the DDA goals of a revived downtown business district. Whirlpool Corporation, always a staunch supporter of anything beneficial to the City, loaned Len Hardtke, who became the professional planner of "Project Foresight." A presentation of slide programs was scheduled at all of the service clubs and other organizations, and the public was made aware and could feel the urgency of our plans for St. Joseph's redevelopment.

Uniquely no money funding was sought from the Federal or State Governments. We were determined to be free of Governmental control and to initiate and complete an entirely local endeavor to save the central business area of the community. The Orchards Mall complex, a multi-million dollar development soon came out of the planning stage and projected the kind of modern, large, indoor mall frequently seen in large urban areas. For St. Joseph it was a case if sink or swim. Fairplain Plaza was doomed to become a weak, stripped secondary mall. St. Joseph had to fight to survive the competition and fight we did.

Over $800,000 was raised by local contributions and corporations, notably Whirlpool and many civic-minded individuals. The business district properties were assessed a special tax. John Stubblefield, President of St. Joseph Improvement Association (SJIA), long term President of People's State Bank and a long time advocate of the revitalization of the St. Joseph Business Corridor, was literally a tower of strength and inspiration for all of us. He contributed very large sums of money to preempt the purchase of the Colonel Wallace home on the southeast corner of State and Elm Streets to make possible, along with property across the street, the construction of critically needed parking at the south end of the proposed State Street renewal project.

The demolition of the Colonel Wallace house was angrily disapproved by many young activists who claimed the house was a historical landmark identified with the early growth of the community. At a heated meeting of the City Commission, my proposal that the best use of the property was to tear it down and pave over the area and adjoining land, also land across the street to provide public parking critically required for the south anchor of the new downtown business area to ensure its success, triggered angry denunciation of Stubblefield and myself. We were figuratively hung in effigy. Heated meetings ensued between proponents of DDA revitalization and those who favored maintenance of the status quo.

Those meetings continued unabated. When we started ripping up State Street to make it a one-way and put in the amenities of trees, live plantings, lamp posts, benches, flower plantings, there were those who complained we were destroying the community.

St. Joseph was coming to life. It wasn't just the central business core of the City that benefited and was being revitalized. It was indeed the whole community, the residents of the entire city who were to recognize ultimately the worth of the efforts to bring new life and vitality to the downtown area. The DDA doctrine early was expressed that if the downtown central business core area could be revitalized and made a pleasant ambient place to shop and do business, St. Joseph's unique location on Lake Michigan would provide the attraction and inducement to make it a culturally alive and exciting center for everyone miles around to enjoy.

We undertook to form and projected a new Chamber of Commerce to represent the business and professional people in St. Joseph. In doing that we recognized that we were to a large extent separating ourselves from the Twin Cities Chamber of Commerce. This was necessary if we were going to have an organization uniquely concerned with St. Joseph. I hosted a meeting at the Berrien Hills Country Club and there a new Chamber of Commerce, appropriately called "St. Joseph Today," was formed with emphasis on the present and future to represent the business and professional people of the city. That organization, with its own Board of Directors and Executive Director (initially Len Hardtke, then Patty Sizer, and her successor, Kathy Zerler), was destined to provide the planning of events, festivals and ongoing affairs which would make the central core of St. Joseph an exciting place to shop and do business.

The whole plan worked. The magnificent Krasl Museum of Art, a generous gift of Olga Krasl, was to rise on Lakeshore Boulevard. The Polansky Library and gardens were to be enlarged and beautified. The beautiful bandshell with its many concerts and affairs, the many festivals - art, antique, venetian and others - promoted by St. Joseph Today were all to have their input in creating a downtown small city ambiance of beauty, vitality and interest and to encourage merchants, professionals and various business interests to be proudly identified with the city.

Visiting officials from communities near and far removed came to St. Joseph and were shown what had been accomplished with local talent, money and resources without the help or interference from the Federal or State Governments. The reaction always was loud acclaim, amazement and appreciation.

The Orchards Mall no longer is a threat to the business interests of downtown St. Joseph. We have held our own proudly, for St. Joseph is a classic prototype of what a small town can do to establish and renew its vitality. The logo formulated by St. Joseph Today is symbolic of that renewed vitality, enthusiasm and beautiful ambiance of a community

which proudly says to one and all:
   "Come see what we have here!"